BIRTH ANGELS

Book of Days

Daily Wisdoms with the 72 Angels of the Tree of Life

Volume 2: June 3 ~ August 16
Relationship with Self

———————————

Terah Cox

Stone's Throw Publishing House
November 2024

BIRTH ANGELS BOOK OF DAYS

Daily Wisdoms with the 72 Angels of the Tree of Life
Volume 2: June 3 – August 16
Relationship with Self

Stone's Throw Publishing House

ISBN-13: 978-0692416907
ISBN-10: 0692416900
Current Edition Softcover: November 2024

For permissions, information about author
and additional books and materials, see
www.72BirthAngels.com
www.TerahCox.com

Book design by Terah Cox | Author photo by Stacie Florer
Wing detail of Fresco Angel by Giotto di Bondone,
  Scenes from the Life of Christ #4 (1304-06)

Vol 2.2_110424

Books by Terah Cox

DIFFERENT SHIPS, SAME BOAT
Songs for the Soul of America: Hurt, Hope, Healing
Words Matter Press (2024)

BIRTH ANGELS BOOK OF DAYS ~ Vols. 1 - 5
Daily Wisdoms with the 72 Angels of the Tree of Life
Stone's Throw Publishing House (Vols. 1-5, 2014-2021)

A LOVE YOUR HEART CAN BELIEVE IN
Stone's Throw Publishing House (2017)

THE STORY OF LOVE & TRUTH
Words Matter Press (2024):
Illustrated Softcover and Hardcover Editions
Stone's Throw Publishing House:
Illustrated Softcover Edition (2011)
Limited Handmade Edition (2007)

BIRTH ANGELS ~ Fulfilling Your Life Purpose
with the 72 Angels of the Kabbalah
Andrews McMeel/Simon & Schuster (2004)
(acquired by Stone's Throw Publishing House 2013)
Greek edition: Asimakis Publishing, Athens, Greece (2014)

YOU CAN WRITE SONG LYRICS
Writers Digest / F&W Publications (2001)

For more information about the 72 Angels tradition,
the Tree of Life, and Birth Angels with Terah Cox:
www.72BirthAngels.com

For permissions, additional works
and information about author:
www.TerahCox.com

Table of Contents

Gratitudes

For this Volume 2 of *Book of Days*, presenting Angelic wisdoms about individuation and relationship with the self, I want to express my deep gratitude for the opportunity to observe and admire the individuation of four remarkable young people in my life—my nieces Hannah Zeno and Bekah Hicks, and goddaughters Lindy and Sara Labriola. It has been a great joy and inspiration to be part of your lives and to watch the unfolding of your beautiful hearts and minds as you have become more and more who you are as artists and creators, each with your unique gifts. Thank you Hannah for being my first love as an aunt, for the privilege of watching you blossom, for the special grace you have always had, the times we have shared and all I have learned from you. And Bekah, thank you for allowing me to come to know you in a whole new way, and to be able to appreciate what an amazing person you have become and are still becoming. Lindy, I am blessed to have been an ongoing participant in your life and to watch the unfolding of your remarkable wise and visionary mind and your talents as a writer, musical and visual artist, and future world-changer. Thank you for our co-creative conversations and the poetry of your uncanny perceptions, as well as for the poem you contributed to this book, our work together, and so much more. And finally, Sara (now Hank), thank you for the delight you have brought to my life in watching you pursue your many musical talents with determination, gratitude, heartfulness, and a quirky natural wisdom that entertains and uplifts everyone around you! Each of you have your own room in my heart, always ready for an impromptu check-in!

Deep gratitude also to friends, family and extended family who have been so supportive and who touch my heart and inspire me again and again with the sparkle of their individualities – Arnie Roman and Tanya Leah, Chuck Pisa, Stacie Florer, the Delzells, Art and Stacy Labriola, Donna Zucchi, Jodi Tomasso, Susan Heiferman, Teri Barr, Teresa Peppard, Honey Kirila, my sisters Connie and Cindy. And finally, much gratitude to Joni Tipping, with whom I've been privileged to come to know and work with on her own book projects and more.

I am also grateful to all who contributed their stories and reviews for this volume, including Jodi Lynn, Sarah Gallant, Aletheia Mystea, Stacie Florer and her beloved late mother, Paula Mooney.

My gratitude list would not be complete without acknowledging all the individuals, retailers and organizations that have been supportive for a number of years in carrying the Birth Angels books and my other works, among them: Aura-Soma Products Ltd., A.R.E. Edgar Cayce Institute, Black Dog Salvage, Book No Further, Booksellers Cincinnati, Country Touch, Crystal Visions, Edenside Gallery, Eclectic Collector Gallery, Elements Spa, Grovewood Gallery, Highland Books, Homestead, Kismet at Caryn's, Kripalu Yoga Center, Local Color, Malaprops, New Mountain Mercantile, Origami Ink, Poor Richards Books, Winter Sun-Summer Moon, Wondrous Things, and so many more.

Thank you all from the bottom and top of my heart.

~ *Terah,* May 2015 – November 2024

* * *

I'm lost, I said, lost.
Soft and sweet she told me, be
A light, lofty and bright
Take on truth and challenge fate
It's only smoke and mirrors.
So I took to the path on foot,
Glancing back behind me now
And again,
To see the lost foes and the lost friends
Who cannot see the light, be the light
Here...now...yet
And I looked ahead and saw a fire
Bright and brilliant, captivating
Filled with promises,
And smoke,
And mirrors.
So I entered the blaze where
Each thing was slightly changed by
The shadows of the leaping flames, but
I measured them against my own light's desire
And I was never lost again.

~ Malinda Labriola

Preface

In my co-creative journey to bring forth the Daily Wisdoms through the five volumes of the *Book of Days*, I have experienced intimately the grace and fluidity of the spiritual within us – how we are so tenderly attended in always being given what we need, even while our willingness and ability to receive is being lovingly supported, sometimes coaxed – but never pushed. Word by word, page by page, this project has beckoned me into the unknown to make it knowable. The more I've been able to receive, the more I've been given, and thus every seeming completion turns out to be another beginning. By the time I was finishing the fifth volume, I knew I must edit the entire series again to reflect my deepening understandings as well as to offer new historical information and clarifications in the tradition that have continued to come to light. In addition, through my ongoing daily review and work with the Daily Wisdoms Email Subscription service, the messages are continuing to be clarified and fine-tuned – and thus, the volumes continue to be updated. Thanks to the new technologies for book publishing, our creations can grow right along with us!

I have gathered years of research into aspects of the Kabbalah from which the 72 Angels tradition emerged. But it is in giving these 72 "angles," or aspects/qualities, of the Divine Light a voice through the Daily Wisdoms that the mysteries of the Divine have been brought more intimately into the "humus" of my own humanity. Possibly the most profound realization I've been led to is that not only is the Divine within us, as us—but even our physical and personality aspects which we think of as human are also Divine. As the second edition of Volume 1 explores, if God is all there is, and all there is *is* God, then there is nothing that is not. Thus the heavier, denser vibrations that compose all matter and form are those aspects of the Divine which enable It to be visible, relatable, diverse and ongoingly creative in ways that can happen only through the physical life.

To really fathom what this means to our humanity, we must address the long-held influences and beliefs that keep us in separate-consciousness about the Divine, ourselves and each other. We must unyoke ourselves from others' notions and definitions of God, "original sin" and all the proprietary claims and dictates of any "only one Truth" that exclude or quash the beauties and sacred purposes of our diversities. We will need to consider, and be willing to see, that God—as the Divine, the All, the cosmic glue, the vibrational fabric of the universe—is within, among and around all of us, expressed and within each of us in unique ways, as the compositional light-stuff of all Creation. And ultimately, we must come to realize that what we do to another IS what we do to ourselves, because essentially, we are all part and expressive of the Oneness, as distinct leaves on the same Tree of Life.

Our relationship with the Divine is at the root of our perceptions about life and relationship with self, which is what Volume 1 explores. And since relationship with self is at the root of our life purposing and relatings with others, in this second volume the Daily Wisdoms support our own heart-and-soul awareness so that we might have access to more of who we truly are and what more we desire to be. Through healing and fulfillment of self, we are able to extend more compassion, kindness, and even inspiration, to others.

As 'light-angles' of the Divine Itself, the 72 Angels reveal the inherent diversity of the Divine expressed within the diversity of our humanity. They help us to cultivate our light-nature in the particular ways that reflect and expand our uniqueness, and they show us how we can use the shadows within as alerts for where healing is needed. For truly, we have come to give form, voice and variation to the Divine's infinite potential to reveal and increase Light in the most dense forms of matter, thought, attitude, feeling, being and doing.

It is amazing to look at ourselves through the loving eyes of the Angels as angles of Divine Light shimmering within and among us. Through these Angelic Lights, we can see our true essential nature as Light. To consider that even the hardest, darkest parts of us are composed of that Light—and to feel heart, mind and body quicken as the Light is increased within us—is to experience what it means to be a Divine-Human being.

Introduction
Our "Image and Likeness" to the Divine

This second volume of the *Book of Days* features wisdoms with the 72 Angels about our most pivotal relationship during our time on Earth—relationship with self. In 72 ways, the Angels share with us in this volume that how we think and feel about ourselves, and the degree to which we are willing to cultivate who we truly are and what we love, profoundly affects how we relate to others and the value we bring to the world. From an inner atmosphere of self-love, acceptance and compassion, we can deepen the roots of Divine Love and Truth within us and in our connections with all of life. Thus when we give the particular gifts of ourselves to the whole—as true individuation aspires to—we, and all others, are not diminished but increased.

Know Thyself. Volume 1 of this series deals with our relationship to the Divine, in which the Angels reveal that our inner longings and outer quests for greater love, meaning and purpose—for something deeper, higher and more fulfilling than the seeming limitations of this life—prevail because our souls are "sparks" of the Divine Itself. This Divine "Light-Stuff" within us carries the imprint and urge of the Divine "I AM" to know and expand Itself—which is echoed in our own great desire to know who we are and what more we can make of ourselves. Through these innermost longings, purposes and urges that compel us our entire lives, we carry "the mark of our Maker."

The more we are willing to sound our own within and to feel and explore our own mysteries, the more we may come to know about the Divine and how Its mysteries are reprised within, and as, us. If we can fathom that, we will have more access to our own totality—not only spiritually, but practically—in ways that can help us to harness all the inner and outer energies available to us so that we might fulfill our dreams and potentials. And importantly, the more we are willing to know the innermost and farthest reaches of ourselves, the more we are willing and able to know the depths of others. We can stop trying to satisfy our longings and quell our boredoms with more and more quantities of people, things and "stuff," and dive into the qualities of feeling, being and doing of ourselves and each other to discover—as William Blake said—"eternity in a wildflower."

What it means to be a Divine-Human being. The 72 Angels describe us again and again as Divine-Human beings. From our cosmic soul-birth to the birth of our soul within human physicality, you might say that here on Earth we are soul and soil—Divine and Human. But the greater truth revealed through the Angel Wisdoms is this, as the Angels SITAEL and ARIEL say in part:

> *We speak of you as Divine-Human beings, and we could also say that you are divinely human, or humanly divine. But the whole truth is that all you are is of the Divine, for there is nothing that is not of God... The light of the sun and the moon, the dust of the stars, the waters and the humus of the Earth, the deep and the dark, the fullness and the void, essence and form— all is Divine. Thus the Divine-Human being that you are is composed of both light and dust, essence and form—the 'stuff' of heaven rooted in the earthly humus of matter ... every part of you fashioned with different frequencies of light, both visible and invisible. ... And so to say that 'the body is a temple of the Divine' is so much truer than you may have ever realized.*

The duality that exists in form is sometimes given a "bad rap" and has certainly been the subject of eons of philosophical and religious argument—often disparaging our human, or "grosser," aspects. In the Angelic realms, however, duality is understood as *"that which enables the interaction of contrasting energies in order to impulse movement and the evolution of consciousness within tangible forms."*

In piecing together the similarities among cosmic and human patterns, the Angelic and ancient wisdoms and the "inner tuitions" that visit me, it is my sense that "in the beginning" duality was both the means and the result of the Divine urge to bring forth Otherness from within Its Oneness in order to know Itself. Thus the One became the many by the emanation of Its own Light into multitudinous colors and qualities which all carried the holographic blueprint of the Divine Itself. Ultimately, through co-creativity among the differentiating and descending frequencies of Divine Light, matter and form were "born," and the I AM was extended into infinitely diverse expressions of "I

AM THAT WHICH... ." Each of these diverse aspects carried, and still carry, a life-urge of its own, with the ability to create from itself further variations in order to proliferate and reflect back to the Divine what more might be created from It, as It.

The beauty of our humanity is that we are composed of many frequencies of that Light—some fine and gossamer-like, as our soul-light, which expresses the higher vibrations of our Divine nature—and others more dense and heavy, like the humus of flesh and bone, in order to provide a grounding container and relatable form for the Light we are, essentially giving our soul "legs to stand on."

The great paradox of ourselves as Divine-Human beings is that the more we awaken to and call upon our inner Divinity and the qualities and powers of Divine Love and Truth within us, the more Divinely, as in *wholly,* human we become. As our humanity is thus Divinely "super-charged" to fulfill our greatest soul purposes and heart-longings—which reflect the desire of the Divine to know what more it can be—we 'go forth and multiply' our wondrous Divine-Human potential through both individuation and togetherness.

The ultimate love-and-truth urge of individuation is to be and create something worthy to contribute to others from the truth of who we are and what we love. The blossoming of our individuation, which is facilitated *because of* our seeming "separation" from our Source, enables us to bring to the whole of humankind, and the Oneness of All That Is, more than we started with. Indeed, when all is said and done, we will hopefully have given our "Light-Seed Investor" a good return on Its investment!

Our ability to do all that hinges on the kind of relationship we have with ourselves, and on our willingness to allow the Divine within us to be the loving co-creator of our lives into greater and greater beingness.

Relationship with Self

In approaching the potential magnitude of who we are, we have to consider that in co-creation with our inner Divine, not even the sky is a limit to what we might become! As the 72 Angels assure us again and again, when we are engaged with cultivating and expressing who we truly and fully are in the commingling of our inner and outer aspects, we are fully supported by the nature of Life itself and Angelically/Divinely/Universally assisted in ways that are most personal and relevant to each of us. But for this support to have full impact, we must get over our discomfort with the concepts of self-love and putting ourselves first.

Ultimately, it is only when we have tapped the limitless power we have within for our own individuation and fulfillment that we will have the fullness of presence to be fully present and also immersed with others, without worry about self-protectiveness or "establishing boundaries." Because only then we will have the *safety* of self-sovereignty that nothing outside of us can breach.

This is what the Heart Angels of Summer are here to help us with in this season when lightness of being and blossoming invite us to the fullness and fruition of our own true colors.

Selfish, Self-ful and Selfless

Selfishness. Among the greatest concerns parents have about the character of their children is that they NOT be selfish. The "terrible two's"—when a child is developing its ego and everything is all about itself and what it wants—is often the most anxious time for parents. Sharing is introduced as soon as "selfishness" starts to rear its head, with disapproval around any insistence of "it's mine!" However, some parenting counselors have suggested that a child will unlearn selfishness naturally, and soon enough, when it begins to be shunned by its own peers for not sharing. Thus the lesson will be learned not through shame, but by the desire to belong and coming to realize the joys and *perks* of reciprocity!

Another vulnerable time in our lives when there is a spotlight on selfishness is during adolescence, when the need to go to another level in our personal individuation is often in direct conflict with the need to be accepted by our peers and have a sense of social belonging. This dichotomy often consumes our teen years, and we can appear selfish or "weird" to both friends and family when we choose our own way over what others want or expect of us.

I will never forget a moment in my childhood when I began to sense the difference between selfish and self-ful, and how suppressed the human spirit can become for fear of being called or thought of as selfish. I was a dreamer from the time I was a little kid, always observing and thinking about the underneath of people and things, the differences between what people said and what they really meant, and about life, love and truth, and wondering where the feeling of "greaterness" inside me came from. Because the world around me was often harsh, I was often in my own world dreaming and thinking, and especially reading, which early on led to going off by myself to write down thoughts and poems. I was thus often accused of having my head in the clouds and being selfish.

I remember how I cringed and felt shame and guilt every time the "selfish" word was flung at me with that terrible tone of derision. One day, when I was about 9 or 10 and I was accused of selfishness yet again, suddenly something inside me pushed back. "I am NOT selfish," I heard myself cry out inwardly. "I'm looking for something *more than* me, but I have to go *through* me to find it." This was probably the first breakthrough of my soul-voice into my consciousness, and it startled me. But from that moment on, I began to listen more and more to that inner voice to drown out the hurtful voices around me.

Years later, through my interest in language, words and root meanings and such, I noted that we use the suffix "ish" to describe many betwixt and between feelings or conditions. And thus it occurred to me that "ish" connected to "self," i.e., "selfish," like the word "childish," describes someone who is *like* a self, or *like* a child, but not actually quite so! Selfish, then, as the Angel Wisdom for YEHUIAH addresses in Volume 1, is something we are when we are not being an authentic self—as opposed to what I call "self-ful," when we are being a full and true self—meaning the self we truly are, and optimally, ever becoming more of.

Ironically, selfishness and selfish acts proceed from us when we have forgotten or feel separate from who we are. Either we're having an alienated moment, or we haven't yet realized or integrated our abundant soul-nature—and therefore we become fearful or protective about not having or being enough. Prolonged, it can lead to a lack of generosity on every level—as well as greed and isolation from the whole and a tendency to approach every encounter from an angle of what that small fearful self can get to keep protecting what little of itself it has.

Despite the high-profile escapades of people who we might describe as chronically *that* selfish, I would speculate that most of us, most of the time, don't go that far down the selfish path. We all naturally have selfish moments and periods here and there because most of us are still learning how to tap the infinitude of ourselves in order to cultivate the joy, fearlessness and fruition of becoming who we truly are. However, part of what impedes us is that we often confuse taking care of ourselves and our own needs, desires and purposes as selfish—and indeed often use that very word as an apologetic when we dare to say no to a request or demand on our time or resources.

Through centuries of programming, this word selfish has instilled shame and guilt and held the individuating self hostage. The word is often used by people who feel diminished and small in their own lives against others who are striving to discover who they are and what their gifts might be—or even against those who just exude enjoyment and self-confidence.

In summary, it is NOT selfish to have compassion and regard for yourself and your own needs, desires and feelings first. It is not selfish to say NO when you really want to. It is NOT selfish to put the needs or demands of others on a back burner when issues in your own life or work are blazing away on the front burner. It is NOT selfish to reject the guilt and blame that others might put upon you as a manipulation to get what they want from you—or to reject the guilt-tape playing in your head that says you won't be a good person if you don't do what someone else needs or wants from you!

YES, we are taught to be considerate of the needs and desires of others, especially our loved ones. As parents we often "sacrifice" for our children when they are young and dependent upon us. But that's not really a sacrifice is it? Isn't it more of a fulfillment of love and caring? But otherwise, generally thinking of others first ultimately only works if everybody is thinking of others first!

It's all about balance—not a balance achieved by every tit-for-tat moment, but the balancing of individuation with togetherness—both of which are necessary for a loving, meaningful life.

Self-fulness. I understand self-fulness as a self-loving way of being in which you can continually evolve toward your authentic and whole self without the constant danger of being fractured by changing circumstances and the beings and doings of others. It might also be called self-possession, self-sovereignty, self-awareness and so on. Self-fulness is not fostered through self-protectiveness, but self-expression and self-trust. It is not self-deprecating, but self-confident. Not self-righteous or self-aggrandizing, but self-respectful. Not self-sacrificial, but self-fulfilling

Self-fulness is "holding your own" with another or in the middle of a crowd—and also having the ability to return to yourself when you have been pulled in different directions, and to put yourself back together when you have become fragmented or over-burdened. Self-fulness is recognizable in people who can renew their equilibrium when life pulls them out of balance. They are generally at ease with themselves and others, and give of their time and talents gladly while also having an unconflicted commitment to what they need and want for their own well-being of person and purpose.

My goddaughter Lindy began to cultivate her self-fulness during high school. She was politically and socially active—joining, running and even founding some of the school's clubs and sports teams. She felt a disconnect, however, between participating in social environments and actually feeling social. Despite being surrounded by gregarious friends and her very sociable sister, Lindy preferred solitude and quiet after school rather than the stress of a constant social agenda in addition to her academic one. Subsequently, outside of classes, club meetings and sport events, she chose to be alone to read, study, write and reflect. Allowing herself to *be* herself not only helped her to meet her academic goals, but prepared her for a college environment in which she was able to connect with true peers. In Lindy's words...

> I never felt lonely in high school. I took pleasure in my own company—but I did feel guilty and selfish for shunning my friends sometimes, preferring the solace and comfort of being alone with my own thoughts. Until college, I never expected to connect creatively or intellectually in the way I enjoyed creating and thinking on my own. When I did enter college, however, I quickly found there were people who understood the way I think, and who were also able to be alone with themselves without feeling badly about it. It was a relief for me to realize that choosing to be alone sometimes is not unhealthy or a selfish rejection of other people's company, but a break from the stress of mainstream life and also a recognition that I simply like to be alone with myself.

> Once I realized that separating myself from everyone for periods of time was healthy and restorative, I was able to become more present with the people that I did spend time with, making the quality and entertainment of conversation even better! It took a change of social context for me to realize that true self-acceptance is not hiding shame about what I could not conform to, but rather embracing what makes me happy, comfortable, and ultimately...myself.

Lindy has learned early in life what so many of us struggle with our whole lives, evidenced by our inner dialogues that start with, "I *should* be/do more..." I would love to see the words *should* and *selfish* disappear from common use toward ourselves and each other at any age—whether used against young people so newly exploring who they are, or those of us who later in life are exploring the possibility of new ways of being, with new purpose and sometimes new people.

My friend Cathleen O'Connor, author, work/life coach and balance guru (thebalancewhisperer.com) says in her wonderful book all about this, *High Heels on the Hamster Wheel*, that the word "no" is one of the most self-loving words in any language when it is used to care for ourselves and improve the quality of our own lives—which, by the way, can ultimately inspire others around us to do the same.

Ultimately, self-fulness, as wholeness, is born from the commingling and cooperation of all one's inner and outer parts which compose the Divine Self and the human self. Even so, self-fulness is not about perfecting yourself, but being willing to be more and more of yourself, without excuse or apology—and yet mindful and responsive to others from the love and truth of who you are. Indeed, the more self-ful, or "full of ourselves" we become—the more we have to give—and actually, the more we *desire* to be of service to others.

Selflessness. For millennia, we have admired remarkable individuals who are held up as role models for their seemingly *selfless* sacrifices for the needs and misfortunes of others, or for some greater good. However, often what may look like a sacrifice to onlookers is actually, to the person who has offered himself or herself, a *fulfillment*. Perhaps we can't imagine "sacrificing" our lives like Jesus, Mother Teresa, Gandhi, the unsung heroes who patrol the back alleys and streets feeding the hungry or taking in the homeless, or the soldier who used to live next door. And maybe thinking of them gives us twinges of not only admiration, but secret shame at our inability to be *that* good.

And so then, what does it mean to be selfless? Is it the "opposite" of selfishness? I say not. It is rather the ultimate capability of self-fulness. Selfless is what we can be when we have enough self inside us that the giving away of it only increases it. When we are finally so comfortable in our own skin that we don't need to erect boundaries or protect ourselves from the "encroachment" of others. Gone is fear for self, the inner judges, the should-would-could inner dialogue, the danger of losing ourselves or being overwhelmed, overshadowed or overruled. We are so at ease with our own beingness, that we can be available to and even immersed in the plight or needs of the other—while instinctively giving ourselves enough restorative time and place.

Selfless is what we can be when we have our inner, eternal resources on tap in such a way that we are given whatever is needed to meet both what we need and desire for our own being, and what we are called to in the service of another. True selflessness is not about

10

martyrdom, though it may look like that to others. Nor is it about being a "doormat" or a "whipping post." Selflessness is possible only when we are able to give unconditionally—because we have no inner need that must be filled by another as payment for our giving. Selflessness comes easily when we are fulfilled by what we do—as if we were born to it.

An everyday example of this is a devoted and loving parent with a sick or hurt child. Or the "good Samaritan" who instinctively rushes in to help someone in sudden danger, even at risk to his or her own life. Or the person who spends years in a laboratory researching a cure for one of our many debilitating diseases, at the expense of a "normal" 9-to-5 work-life or even family, friends and fun-filled vacations.

We must consider that the selfless beings who have graced our lives and our human histories chose to offer their own lives, each in their own ways—some even unto death—as a fulfillment of their personal sense of purpose. Let us admire and be grateful to them, and to the wonder of the diverse expressions and capacities of our humanity. But let's do that without comparing ourselves to them— even when we are inspired because of them to a selfless moment, or purpose, in our own lives.

The Angels and all that is of Spirit tell us that the holiest thing each of us can do is to be truly and wholly who we each are as a unique soul-spark of the Divine carrying out our own particular Divine-Human purposes. We are not here to be anyone else or to follow a star in someone else's sky. We are here to be someone no one else can be. This is the self-fulness that eclipses self*ish*ness in both time and eternity. And the more self-ful we become, if there comes a time when we are called to an extraordinary selflessness, we will be ready without question or self-concern.

Becoming Full of Ourselves

I remember being in a diner one Easter Sunday brunch with a group of people when a woman walked in outfitted in a large colorful hat with a big feathery flower, a fiery royal blue dress and a spirit to go along with it all. She was magnificent and her self-enjoyment was an instant inspiration to me! We all looked up at her as she walked by, and then someone at my table said something I have heard so many times, "Hmmph! She really thinks she's something, so full of herself!" Before I could conjure compassion for the critic, the Scorpio in me uttered a flippant remark, "She IS something, and *who else* should she be full of *anyway*?" No one at the table had anything more to say about it!

The Daily Wisdom with MITZRAEL says: *It doesn't make you bigger to make others smaller so that you don't have to feel your own smallness.* The instant we stop allowing our own lack of self-worth to diminish others, and dare to admire them instead, we are enlarged with new dignity and our own infinite possibility quickens.

I sense that when we feel small and afraid (and most of us do at one time or another), it is because we are actually living—or even behaving for a moment—as partial, and thus smaller, versions of ourselves. That something-like-a-self I spoke of above which can take us into selfishness. This happens when we are not going through life on all 4 cylinders—our spiritual, emotional, mental and physical parts—that together enable the creative engine that takes us through our lives to be working at full throttle. As human beings, born with spiritual amnesia and a vague sense of displacement and existential longing, we can so easily feel small, powerless and overwhelmed. And this becomes especially acute if we do not know how to (or that we even could) reconnect with our own limitless inner resources of heart and soul.

As the Angels show us again and again, the vibrancy of our own individual beingness is dependent upon the interconnectedness of the inner and outer parts that our wholeness is composed of: soul, heart, mind and body. A clue to this is in the word "indivi-duality"— indicating that our *duality* as an inner-outer, Divine-Human being is and must be *indivisible,* or undivided, for the optimum well-being and fulfillment of our totality. Thus, to individuate is to become true, full, whole and undivided within and as ourselves—full of ourselves, in a state of *self-fulness.* Then, when we give ourselves away to others and to our own creations, as true individuation aspires to, we, and all others, are not diminished but increased.

An important thing to realize about becoming a whole and full self is that it is not a static arrival point, a *fait accompli* that once achieved is done and now we can move on to something else. For as the wise have told us for eons, life is not so much a time and place for arriving as it is for journeying. Our journey toward self-fulness is exercised within new scenery and with new or newly-becoming people and circumstances every day. And thus our self-fulness must be renewed every day from one moment and encounter to another by balancing the needs and demands of our outer world with our inner loves, truths, needs and desires.

Balance is not always achieved in the moment, and as author Cathleen O'Connor says, neither is it about "equal time." Sometimes we are called to excessive work hours to meet a deadline or we must drop everything to attend to a loved one who is ill or in great need, or we are pulled this way and that by various urgencies that pop up on any given day. Our willingness to be present and responsive, rather than resistant, to what is needed in the present eases the stress of those times—especially if we know that we will ultimately do what is needed to restore and care for ourselves.

Being able to live in the balance of individuation and togetherness is learning how to modulate the pull of the world with the purposeful presence of the soul—what Buddhism calls mindfulness, or Ram Dass to "be here now." What is so potent about being present is that it is the threshold into the eternal—the realm of our soul with its lifeline to Spirit and a way of being in which we have all the time and timelessness we could ever need. In presence, we can experience the Truth that our innermost nature—our personal "I Am," is revealed and expanded only by Love—and from Love comes all our potential fullness of being and the infinite All we can access to give unto others.

Being Present, Being Love

I remember throwing myself desperately and dramatically across my bed one afternoon years ago and crying out, "Oh God, where are you?!" Silence. "Oh well," I sighed and sank down into the bed a little deeper. Just then I heard a chuckle, of the cosmic kind. And then a voice with a hue of levity answered me, "I AM HERE. WHERE ARE

YOU?" Startled, and then laughing, I realized of course that I had been everywhere *but* here, and that likely all the desperation I was feeling was just the flailing of someone who had lost her way to the present, where my lifeline to the Divine as my greater inner resource was dangling unutilized.

The popular phrase (and title of a book by Jon Kabat-Zinn) "wherever you go, there you are" is a testament to what is always an opportunity but can also feel like a no-escape hatch! On the one hand, our ability to still be here, still standing or willing to get back up, while people and things come and go in our lives, is our salvation. On the other hand, while at times we may try to escape or dull some painful part of ourselves—it's true—here we still are, perhaps suffering even moreso for trying to run away! Although what we are running from may be some aspect of our behavior or our life that we hold shame, guilt or judgment against—we cannot isolate, run from or banish any one part of ourselves without diminishing the vitality of our entire being.

Presence is a come-as-you-are party. As the Angel Wisdoms tell us again and again, by loving, accepting and including every part of who we are right now as vital parts of our whole—even while we are striving to become the "more and better" of who we want to be—ultimately we can "love into being" our own greatness.

So how do we get there, or rather, all the way *here*?

One of the gifts in working with the 72 Angels is learning our way back to the present from yesterday and tomorrow and the constant demands on our attention from moment to moment. I have had to practice this hundreds of times in the writing and rewriting of these five volumes. The outer world and my relentless to-do list were often pitted against my ability to stay present with the Angelic Energies and their messages in a state of love and presence. Staying present all the time was simply impossible. The key, I finally learned, was not in *staying* present, but *returning* to the present.

Because of the constant demands and responsibilities of human life, most of us simply cannot retain a continual state of love and presence. Rather we must keep *renewing* it every day, moment to moment and from one encounter and conversation to the next. As frustrating as this can be—because we want to have *arrived* already— it has helped me to understand that the process of becoming who we truly and fully are is not meant to be an arrival, but an ongoing journey of return to the love-and-truth *isness* of ourselves in any scenario.

Although our personal cycles of ebb and flow and our daily "prodigal journeys" may seem like our human foibles, I have realized how valuable even irritating interruptions, delays and detours can be in providing information and perspective on both our work and ourselves. Even when we are doing something we love, we need contrast, complement and confirmation—and the perspective that "time away" often gives us.

Our inner-outer dance. The Angels convey, each with their particular qualities, how to continually bring our inner and outer back together into presence—not with a constant push and pull between them, but as a kind of Divine-Human "pas de deux" that allows each to lead at different times according to the rhythm, and needs, of the moment or circumstance. All the parts that compose our inner and outer are necessary to the vitality and wholeness of who we are. When we harbor self-judgment, shame, doubt or guilt we tend to ostracize and suppress certain aspects of ourselves. When that happens, we are no longer in the present, where all things are possible.

The Angel Wisdoms tell us that having all our inner and outer parts come together in presence is done through our **willingness** to come within and receive **love, compassion and forgiveness** for ourselves—and to use the parts of ourselves that are stronger in any given moment to help our hurting or weaker parts and moments. A simple example would be to let yourself stay home and not go to the party if you're feeling ill, vulnerable or the need for quiet—instead of being guilted into going because your friend doesn't want to go by herself, or your boss or family is expecting you. Another example would be to take your mind for a sunny walk in nature when it's feeling cloudy, or to sit on a park bench or take a nap in the middle of the day. Or letting your logic throw you a "flotation device" when you're drowning in emotional overwhelm. Or taking a break from a certain person who pushes buttons you're not quite ready to address, or finding a gentler, kindler classroom for things you need to learn.

The willingness to go within and listen to what all our parts need cultivates a softness that strengthens us. From our own within we give our outer expressions and powers meaning, purpose and the commitment to go any distance we have set for ourselves. In our willingness to realize and co-create with the Divine that is already within every aspect of our being, we need never be held hostage to outer circumstances, seeming limitations or others' expectations.

And finally, going within puts us in the presence of the Presence that not only helps us to be fully present, but also takes us from the present into the eternal—where all that we need to both withstand and fulfill our experience of time and place is given to us, if we are willing to receive.

Finding Our Way Within

We are pulled within most dynamically, perhaps, by our feelings. Feeling of any kind can open and awaken us, but it's usually the emotions of pain and grief which most capture our attention. However, pain itself is only a pointer, an "usher" to take us across the threshold from the outer to the inner. Pain can bring us from our reactive emotions to a deeper part of the heart, to the place where the light of that which knows who we are is waiting to lead us the rest of the way into, and out of, our suffering. That light is love, and the truths that it reveals and grows. For only love sees the whole truth of us that is beyond what we may be suffering in the moment

With our busy outer lives, we often wait until we're in pain to go within. But if we cultivate a strong inner life, and bring that into our daily life of being and doing, we will be better equipped to handle *everything*. When hurts happen, we can learn how to follow our emotions to their causal source and mine the deeper resources of our heart for understanding and healing. The more engaged we become with the extraordinary resources of our own within, we will be better able *in the moment* to recognize and receive the gifts in the challenges and difficulties that life and the deeper work of our soul bring to us.

In building an inner life, it helps to be aware of what takes us within, effortlessly and joyfully—and to remember to partake of it *daily*! For many, it is prayer or meditation, sleep, dreaming, or doing something we truly enjoy. I am immediately drawn inward when I am reading, writing or being in nature. My engagement with the natural world after years of city living opened up "al fresco atriums" in my own within that I didn't even know were there.

There is something in the beauty and sentient presence of nature that calls to the deepest levels of our own. I haven't found any simpler, quicker or more beautiful way to go within than to go out into nature. Sitting or walking meditations, reading, writing and ruminating while surrounded by the soft whisperings of trees and the melodies of birdsong can be so much more profound than when done indoors. For me, one walk down a forest path and all my worldly shields fall away as I am felt, heard and somehow inwardly tended by the forest presences.

To be amidst all the different textures, sounds and scents of nature is to be reminded of our own natural beauties. To look up at the branching of the trees into an infinite sky is to be reminded of the sky of our own hearts, ever dreaming and reaching. To walk in the quiet of a winter snow, and encounter a deer or other creature who stops to look right at us, is to realize that we have suddenly been met by the visible Divine Other on our path...and the sound of Amen resounding within and all around us.

One of the wonderful things about going within is that we are also met by the unseen "Others" that attend and watch over us. Thus, not only our own soul and other-world guides meet us within, but also the greater Spirit that sustains our soul as part of the totality of All That Is addressing the particularity of who we are in this life, in this moment. Whether we understand this meeting and communion to be with a particular guide, the collective voice of our ancestors, the "Ascended Masters," Christ, Buddha, our "guardian Angels" or the Angelic as/or the Divine Itself—what is common to all spirit-presentations of our inner other(s) is the conveyance of love. And their love is not just directed at us or for us, but to give us an experience of what love feels like *as us*.

Two Sufi poets, Rumi (13th c.) and Hafiz (14th c.), come to mind whose works are saturated with the mystical love of what Rumi calls the "inner Beloved...knocking from the inside." (*The Illuminated Rumi*, p. 37). The possibility for mystical union with our "inner Beloved" is also found in the lives of some of the saints—St. Teresa of Avila and St. John of the Cross come to mind, as well as mystic poets such as William Blake, Emerson, Wordsworth, even Emily Dickinson at times. When you read certain works of these visionaries, you feel not only the other-worldly love they describe, but the altered state of their own beings as if they are the thing, the love itself, with voice and presence. But you don't have to be an artist or poet to experience this.

What we can come to realize in our own inner depths is that even before love is a feeling or an action verb, love is something more foundational. Love is one part of our ISNESS—the part that recognizes, increases and evolves our other part, which is the truth of who we are, in both time and eternity. Working with the 72 Angels has helped me to understand that. If indeed we are rendered in the "image and likeness" of the Divine I AM, then the role of love within us is to illuminate the I Am of our particular uniqueness—the personal "I am that which" that describes who we are as a soul-body, Divine-Human being expressing a particularity of the Divine on Earth. And thus, it is our sacred task, for the sake of both the Divine which we are here to express and the earthly fulfillment of our soul, to allow love to bring the greater truth of who we each are into full beingness.

And so, as the Wisdoms suggest, for every dream you dream, every question you have, whatever truth you seek and whatever inner or outer challenge you face, consider that the answer and the solution is love—and look to what love is calling you to in that moment.

The Cultivation of Self-love

Self-love is essentially the Divine loving us from the inside, inviting us to embrace the Divine-Human totality of who we are both in and out of time. In learning to love the whole of ourselves as we are loved by the Divine, we become aware that the Divine is the co-creator of our human life, that who we are and what we love matters because we are here to discover, express and share the love and truth of who we are as a particular expression of the Divine on Earth. The Wisdom of JELIEL puts it this way:

> *Loving yourself is not a selfish thing—it is necessary in order to live truly and rightly in your world and to bring forth loving creations and relationships. The key is in knowing and feeling that you are a unique expression of the Divine Self and Its desire to experience life and love through you in the ways only you can. Just as you are loved by That Which created you, love and care for yourself and your own creations. There is no question of your worthiness when you understand that your true lineage is of the Divine Itself. 'The apple does not fall far from the tree' because the apple contains the tree within it.*

We are used to thinking of love in the context of otherness—how we feel about another or how they feel about us. And so while it may not be easy to feel *self*-love, we can create an environment that supports the cultivation of it. I have found these three things to help: self-acknowledgment, self-acceptance and self-care.

Self-acknowledgement. With this humble beginning, you observe, admit and define what you are feeling, wanting, doing and being—without self-judgment or criticism. You can do this in your own head and heart or with some simple list-making—or you can ask someone to witness your declaration of self-acknowledgment. Acknowledge what you like and don't like about yourself. And acknowledge who you are without regard to who you or someone else may have ever thought you should be. To truly see and know yourself as you are *now* can cast a different light on your past. Your past self and circumstances are not entirely causal and responsible for who you are now. In that formative mix is also an ongoing sense and affinity for who you have wanted to become—and the choices you have made in every present moment toward that future self. Often when we bring our past, present and future selves into the same consciousness space, we find that we have harbored notions about ourselves from years ago that are no longer even true, and we can let them go.

I once experienced in a seminary workshop a wonderful exercise to invoke the power of acknowledging the things about ourselves we don't like, things that can lurk and linger in our inner shadows—and dispel them with humor and humility. We were asked to think of someone we had issues with and make a list of three character traits that most annoyed us about that person. And then we were asked to introduce ourselves to the people around us as if we ourselves embodied those traits—for example, "Hello, I am selfish, boring and arrogant. How are you today?" And the other person might answer, "Hello, nice to meet you. I am fearful, suspicious and argumentative." Very quickly we were all laughing as we realized two important things: (1) Our issues with others often reflect issues we have with ourselves, and (2) we've all got some work to do!

Funny how "humor" and "humility" have the same root as "human." To put humor in the place of judgment of self or others is to invite both levity and compassion into the musty corners of harbored hurts and guilts within us, giving us an opportunity to chase the boogey-man of the "self-who-should-not-be-named" out from our inner closets of judgment and shame. This unleashes the power that is the underpinning of self-acknowledgment: that whatever truth we are clinging to (personal truths of self or others) is not absolute, i.e., static or fixed, but relative—because love is always, *always,* freeing truth (and us) to evolve into a new truth. Therefore, speaking the truth of who we are or how we feel or what we want in any given moment does not define us indefinitely, but rather locates us in the "what is" of time so that we can take the next step toward "what will be" in our ever-new becoming. That next step is self-acceptance.

Self-acceptance is about being more at ease in allowing ourselves to be who we are right now, inside and out, while working on who we want to be. With self-acceptance we can use missteps and mis-takes as test-runs for learning and doing it better the next time. If we focus on the journey—the "out-go," rather than the outcome— we will come to know that each time we are willing to take a small step forward, a quantum leap is made in both our inner and outer journeys.

When we resist who or what we don't want to be, we are stewing in self-judgment and focused on what we *don't* want. But when we stop *shoulding* all over ourselves, we are free to start accepting and maybe even enjoying who we are in this moment—knowing that we're still journeying, still becoming, because our story is still unfolding. This is so important because we can only get to whoever, whatever and wherever else we want to be from here and now. We can't launch from the "land of should" because it doesn't yet exist. It's like trying to take a next step when your legs are spread so far apart that when you try to move forward, you just fall. That's the point of that popular cliché about making sure we have both feet under us when we're trying to get ourselves to the next place. It's really just a metaphor for the "wherewithal" of all our parts being in the present, which is always our point of greatest power. And the best way to get our wherewithal ready for anything is through self-care.

Self-care. Self-care is important at all four levels of our being and involves both will and *willingness*. We are not a jumble of unrelated parts, as western medicine is having to more and more acknowledge. Each aspect of who we are affects every other part of us. Thus, to disregard any of our parts—**physical**, **mental**, **emotional** or **spiritual**—for any length of time will cause the others to weaken.

(1) **Physical self-care** often gives immediate results which also accumulate over time into a greater degree of overall well-being: (a) Eat healthy, nutritious food for at least the majority of your daily diet; (b) Exercise, i.e., move your body, every day—whether through walking, running, working out, swimming, dancing or whatever you can do that you *will* do, and enjoy; (c) Get the rest and sleep you need.

The best way to maintain these is to do them from a sense of purpose rather than guilt. Set some routines or schedules for yourself, and <u>choose</u> to break out of them sometimes so that you don't make a taskmaster of yourself. Enjoy both doing them and not doing them, knowing that you will return to the doing the next day, or soon. You will experience a beautiful dignity and power in the choosing that will support a sense of purpose and an honoring of yourself. And importantly, you will learn to appreciate process and how effective regular practice can be as you come to see the changes in your physical, emotional and mental well-being that do come.

(2) **Mental self-care** is about awareness and mindfulness, but also allowing the intuition and wisdom of your heart to inform your thoughts. When you are cut off from the eternal resources of your heart, your thoughts can become rampant and chaotic, self-defeating, and at the very least debilitating and *limiting* the powers of all the rest

of your parts. By engaging your intellect in work, activities, pastimes and pleasures that are stimulating to not only your intellect but also to a sense of meaning and purpose, your mental powers are vastly increased.

(3) **Emotional self-care** is about inner equilibrium and outer encouragement and support. When you cultivate an overall feeling for your life that comes from your sense of personal truth and what you love and desire for your life, reactive and temporary emotions are less likely to become "the tail that wags your dog." As "hue-man" beings we both delight in and suffer from a multitude of colorful emotions, which can change on a dime from one to the other and range from the highest highs to the lowest lows. But if we do not overidentify with our reactive emotions, letting them literally 'get the best of us,' then we may not only see, but be able to move beyond those temporary emotional buffetings to our deeper, more stable feelings about self, others and what truly matters to us.

There is sometimes a chicken-or-egg debate as to which is more causal to our life conditions—emotions or thoughts. Throughout the latter third of the 20th century, positive-thinking and self-help proponents focused on the rehabilitation of our thoughts and repetition of mental affirmations to help us effect change and improve our lives. But thoughts are hard things to change or control without input from our other parts, especially as our thoughts are often driven by hurts and other life experiences that are harbored, even hidden, deep inside us. This can cause us to attract the very opposite of what we want, no matter how much we may think and affirm what we want in our thoughts. If we harbor a deeper ongoing feeling or belief that we don't deserve it, or that we can't have it because of one reason or another—then we are attracting *not* getting it because we are vibrationally broadcasting lack.

This is because the law of attraction works in a way that attracts situations and outcomes that match our *feelings* and the vibrations they emit. In addition, underneath our feelings there is another causal factor, which is the composite of our core beliefs and judgments about ourselves.

There are so many things, circumstances and people that can affect our core beliefs in both life-affirming and life-negating ways, and they usually start in early childhood and can accumulate like a snowball rolling downhill throughout our lives. In essence our core beliefs color our perceptions and our thoughts, including whether we experience life as supportive or unsupportive of our potentials, purposes, dreams and endeavors—which affects how we feel about ourselves. Thus, emotional self-care includes the willingness to examine our self-beliefs and seek healing for any chronic feeling or perception that is undermining us. In addition, observation of our thoughts and feelings, as well as physical ailments, can be used as clues to where there are distortions in our core beliefs and where we might begin our healing.

All of the above is easier said than done. And that's where the preciousness of relationship comes in. The English metaphysical poet John Donne (16th century) wrote, "No man is an island entire of itself..." One of the most important things we can do in life is to keep company with people who see and appreciate who we truly are and encourage what more we desire to become. These are the people who help to shine a light back to ourselves when we seem to be wandering astray, the ones who remind us of what we already know but may have forgotten for a time. The ones who see and believe in the best within us. The ones who help us to reclaim our strength and integrity of self when we feel weak or uncertain. We cannot be our best self alone. Yet our best relationships are not about staving off loneliness; they are about co-creating our lives with each other in the kind of mutual support and caring which inspires us to grow, dares us to dream, to love, and to do life in ways that are guided by the ever-unfolding truth of who we are. Any relationship that is not doing this is likely one that is showing us the discomfort or hurt inside us that needs healing.

(4) **Spiritual self-care** is about acknowledging, at the very least, that there is more to ourselves, each other and all of life than meets the eye. While many may feel that a spiritual life involves adherence to the rituals and dogmas of a particular religious tradition, here I am talking about something much more intimate and personal than religious dogma.

Essentially, spiritual self-care is about soul-awareness and realization of the spiritual lifeline of "more" which dangles in every encounter, conversation and circumstance. It is about the paradoxical power of willingness over willfulness, surrender over control, trust over worry, faith over fact, and the grace that can bring far greater transformation and healing than any discipline, endeavor, expertise or excellence can effect.

Spiritual self-care involves *regular* engagement in what deepens your life with a sense of meaning, purpose, and presence. Your spiritual practice may be daily rituals of prayer, chanting or meditation, reading, writing, drawing, listening to music or walking in nature. It may simply be a moment's stillness with the dawn's unique sunrise before starting your day, or stopping your work to watch how sunset colors the sky and brings on the beauties of night.

In whatever ways you attend to the soul within you and the eternal and invisible co-creative energies and presences which support your visible being and outer world, know that they are there— *here*—to help and support you in creating the life and love you so deeply desire at every level of your being. However heavy your life circumstances may seem at times, when you allow the resources of your soul to weigh-in on the other three aspects of your being, your heart will be truer and lighter, your mind less encumbered, and your body freer and healthier.

Banishing original sin. One of the most important aspects of self-love is to banish the notion of "original sin," in whatever form it lurks in your life. Original sin, as a religious concept, implies that we are natively and irrevocably tainted. It hovers in the background of personal and social morality, even if we are not religious, and shame and guilt are its offspring.

We don't come to Earth to be knotted up in shame and guilt. We come to show how the light of love and truth can find its way into the darkest, densest and lowest vibrations of thought, feeling, matter and behavior—and that with the quickening of this light within us we can rise to our greatest possibilities.

I like Trappist monk Thomas Merton's definition of sin linked to its Latin origin, meaning "without." Merton wrote in *New Seeds of Contemplation* (1933) that sin is simply that lesser thing we do when we have forgotten who we are and act as if we are without God, and therefore, without the truth of our own nature (paraphrased).

In realizing our inherent goodness—on our way to embracing our "*godness*"—we become free to make whatever course-corrections are needed in the denser vibrations of physical life in order to bring us back to the light of love and truth that we essentially are. So don't let shame and guilt linger, the 72 Angels encourage us. When they show up, use them as a prompt for setting things right, and then move on! To be intimidated by shame and guilt, and the self-judgment that follows, only impedes personal "at-onement," individuation and the sharing of one's unique self and gifts with the world.

Transformation of consciousness is ongoing, and the attainment of enlightenment is daily renewable—but we came equipped! For here in the heart of us each and all is where our "base mettle" is transformed into the gold of Divine-Human beingness. Here, at this inner "grail-altar" where our Divine and human aspects meet and commingle, we are offered the cup of life's mysteries daily. And as we drink from this cup-of-many-flavors every day, inner thirst may be quenched and all our parts replenished and renewed.

One day you may be walking along, or waking up, or noticing the beautiful day—and suddenly—there will be a feeling that wells up from within that is something like joy for no particular reason. Something like peace, even in the middle of a crowd. Something like a deep and serene gladness for just being alive. It will be love, loving you from your own inside.

As the Wisdom of JELIEL puts forth:

> ...*Love yourself, and you will be loving the Divine within as we love you. Love yourself, and you will draw others who will love you. Love yourself, and you will inspire others to love their own beautiful beings as well. Ask any question, seek any purpose, and the answer will be the same: Love, and the heart-truth that love reveals, which is that you are made of love. This is the wisdom of life.*

In summary, with a cumulative daily practice of incorporating self-acknowledgment, self-acceptance, and self-care, we cultivate not only our earthly self-awareness—but also an awareness of our greater Divine-Human Self. We become more able to move ourselves through life and all that the world offers and serves up to us with more joy, more buoyancy, more energy for our own dreams and goals—and a "light-bearer" not only for ourselves, but also for all those whose lives we touch—whether they be loved ones, colleagues or "strangers of consequence."

Daily Life with the 72 Angels

Throughout the co-creating of the Daily Wisdoms, I have experienced in my own life, and observed in others, the power of daily practice with the 72 Angels in awakening our heart-and-soul awareness, which sets the stage for our ongoing transformation. Since the Daily Wisdoms feature messages with the Angels when they are each in their 'heart dominion' as the day's Heart Angel, they remind us to "come from our heart" wherever we go and to bring our inner Divine along to whomever we meet and whatever we do. Thus, as we proceed through the seasons of our life from a heart-centered approach, we are able to mine the spiritual gold in every relating and situation and share it with others in the winding ways of our life journey.

I have often taken issue with the Eastern concept—or the common understanding (or misunderstanding) of it—that life is "maya," or illusion. In my work with the Angelic energies, I have come to feel that this plane of existence is NOT an illusion, but a vibrant, ever-evolving context. An experience, a way of being that allows every aspect of the inherently diverse Divine to manifest with a life and beingness of its own—at the same time, paradoxically, as part of the totality—like leaves on one great family tree of creation. What is an illusion is to think that this world's reality, or our own visible beingness, is *all* there is—or that our perceptions, feelings and thoughts are our only reality.

As the Angel Wisdoms like to say, sometimes a leaf is so far out on a branch that it has forgotten the trunk that supports it, the roots that sustain it, and the heart-sap that nourishes it. It's just out there waving in the wind, catching the light, shining with all its changing colors through the seasons of life. Nevertheless, for all its own forgetting, it is not forgotten by the tree itself as it continues to be sustained for all its days. And then the day comes when its form falls to the ground to become nutrients for the soil that nurtured and rooted it. Suddenly it is no longer contained and constricted in form, and its essence is freed to remember that however magnificent it was to be a leaf, it is now, and once again, far more than it was as a leaf-form. For its greater life—its essential life—is eternal.

It is precisely to remind and help us to partake of our own inner eternal nature that the 72 Angels are given as our Divine allies and continual loving support for all our days. And to realize that we are a precious and unique expression of the Whole, and that through all our seasons of change during and after this life our essence shall be gathered back in and nurtured until we are ready to take on the world again!

The Alchemy of Angelic Awareness

As Volume 1 presents, awareness is key to our awakening, deepening and ongoing Divine-Self realization. Because physical life constantly pulls us toward form, matter and the outer world, the Daily Wisdoms are given to awaken and renew awareness of our spiritual nature on a daily basis. Using the Wisdoms to prompt our awareness attracts opportunities for us to work with and incorporate the specific Divine qualities which the day's Angel energetically embodies. We come to realize that there is so much more to see than we are looking at, so much more to feel and know than what has been handed down to us by others. Over time, we learn to utilize our magnificent inner resources, including the soul-voice within our hearts and our Angelic support system, as inner allies and the agents of our healing and transformation.

Welcoming the Angels. As we invite the Angels to take up more of our inner room, there is less space for doubts, fears, guilt, shame and old hurts—and more room for the truth of who we are and the self-love that enables us to truly love others. Our endeavors become less effort-full as we resist less and less the events, things and people in our everyday world. We see the opportunities waiting in the wings of every moment, and in coincidental encounters and conversations that offer uncanny and timely messages. More and more our daily lives become full of signs, wonders, symbols and clues to unlock the meanings and purposes of our gifts, potentials and challenges as we are paradoxically empowered by our inner Divinity to become more fully and wholly human.

28

Through the 72 Angels we come to understand that we each exist as a uniqueness of possibility, being and expression within the Divine Oneness, and that the Divine exists within, and as, us in order to express and experience life as only each of us can live it. Thus, when we welcome the Angels as *angles*, or qualities, of Divine Light—we do not do so as if they are separate from, or above, us. What we are actually doing is quickening our awareness to see that they are already here within and around and among us. And it is our awareness which activates and amplifies their energies within us—similar to the cosmic law of attraction, which increases what we give our attention to. And thus, by welcoming the Angels, we acknowledge our willingness to engage their Divine magnificence shimmering within us *as our own potential.*

The 3-step path of Angel-alchemy. As in the Divine-Human mysteries of many spiritual paths, we are invited to three things in our work and play with the Angels: **ask**, **receive** and **become**. This ongoing 3-step "Angel-alchemy" can transform our base *mettle* into the spiritual gold of Divine-Human consciousness and a life uniquely fulfilled in manifested love, truth and eternal wisdom.

1. **Ask** (Invoke)—Pray/chant/speak the Angel's name, open your heart and invite its presence to expand within you.

2. **Receive** (Imbibe)—Breathe in, listen, meditate upon and allow the Angel's essence and energy to expand within your heart and being.

3. **Become** (Embody)—Absorb, digest and assimilate the Angel's qualities into the very belly of your beingness so that your awareness and action come into harmony (as in "walking the talk").

These steps can be part of a meditation with the day's Angel and used to focus attention and awareness for everything you encounter during your day. The effects of using these steps for a few minutes daily, or even situationally, begin to accumulate and grow exponentially within you as you keep renewing your awareness. And as relationship with your own inner Divine deepens, you will come to trust the truth-voice in your heart as the guidance of soul and Spirit in the great and small moments of your life.

Ultimately, as the Angels quicken their particular aspects of Divine Light, Love and Truth within us, the greater love and truth of who we are is revealed and magnified and we are better able to see ourselves, each other and all of life in a greater Divine-Human co-creative light.

Ways of Working with the 72 Angels

Work and play with the 72 Angelic Energies is about much more than invoking Angels as guardians and protectors. As "refractions," or "angles" of the Divine Light and Being, they are regarded by Kabbalists not as creations of the Divine, but as differentiated aspects of the Divine Itself—what has been referred to in certain ancient works, as well as in the Old Testament of the Bible, as "Angels of the Presence," and in the Kabbalah Tree of Life mysteries as "the Divine in detail," as well as "the 72 Names [and Faces/Qualities] of God."

As particular qualities of the Divine "I AM" working within, and as, the qualities of your own human "I Am," the role of the 72 Angels in your life is to bring soul-awareness into your daily being and doing and to help you harness the spiritual powers of love to reveal and grow the truth of who you are. They do this not only with love and compassion, but also with lightness and humor, surprise and serendipity!

In both the short and the long run, being and expressing your true self is fundamental to having a nurturing and productive relationship with yourself and others, your work and purpose, and the greater world. In this way you may experience the fulfillment of your unique Divine-Human potential as infinitely more than the sum of your parts. In addition, the Divine Itself may experience what more can be made of It through the more you have made of yourself.

The intent of the medieval and Renaissance Kabbalists who cultivated and carried this wisdom through the centuries was to provide practical spiritual tools for awakening the mysteries of the Divine within our humanity. That said, you don't have to know anything about the tradition to partake of the Angelic Energies or their Wisdoms. Just receive their messages at the altar of your own heart, and let their work begin. Slowly, subtly, sometimes epiphanously, the details and demands, challenges, purposes and potentials of your everyday life are eased, transformed and ennobled.

While your experiences with the Angelic Divine will be unique to you, provided below are some practices that can help to engage the Angelic Energies in your life:

(1) **Work with the Angel of the day** to set your awareness for a particular Divine Energy which you can draw on to support, and even transform, the details, encounters and events of your day. Using the three-step alchemy path to invoke and meditate on the day's "Heart Angel" can be a powerful way to set a particular spiritual tone for your day. In addition, gathering some quiet time for a few moments at the beginning of each day to read and contemplate the Daily Wisdom (using either the *Book of Days* or the Daily Wisdoms email subscription) can also spiritually jump-start your day by helping to renew your awareness, and thereby draw opportunities throughout the day for you to practice the very qualities that the day's Angelic Energy represents and supports.

Since the daily message is meant to speak to your heart, you may find that you are inspired, or challenged, to approach yourself and others more heartfully—as in more lovingly, truly and wisely. Pay attention to the moments that resonate or trigger a feeling or reaction of any kind, which will indicate a timely and specific relevance to you. For example, let's say the Angel of the day is NEMAMIAH, who is all about the discernment of heart-seeing. On NEMAMIAH's day of support, you may find yourself in scenarios that invite you to temper a "rush to judgment" by using the greater seeing of your heart to consider underlying factors of cause or motivation. If you are a parent, you may be moved to exercise compassion rather than discipline in order to discover why your child is behaving in a certain way. If you are a business owner, you may realize before you implement certain improvements that it might be expedient, and respectful, to consult the employees who actually do the work in that area. If you are a doctor or a healer of any kind, you might draw on the energy of discernment to make a connection between your patient's emotional or mental state and their physical ailment.

For more deliberate work, you may want to <u>keep a daily journal</u> of Angelic signs, happenings, coincidences, "inner tuitions," feelings, thoughts and prayers. And if something unusual or interesting occurs, or perhaps you have an important meeting, you may want to note the Intellect Angel governing at that time to prompt awareness and inner support. (See Appendix I for a list of the Angels in their 20-minute periods of intellect support.)

In using any of these practices on a daily basis, I and many others have noticed that correspondences with the particular Angelic energies at play in the day's happenings seem to increase. I believe that is because: (1) as the law of attraction shows us, whatever we give our attention to increases, and (2) "all roads lead home"—we are always met by the Divine in whatever path and vocabulary of our choosing. Thus by incorporating the 72 Angels into our spiritual language or pathworking, the Divine within us communicates to us in an Angelic context.

(2) **Work with your personal Birth Angels** to help you realize: (a) your soul-identity, (b) which aspects of the Divine you are here to particularly manifest in this life, and (c) how to use the eternal resources of the Angelic Divine within you to "supercharge" your human beingness and help you to fulfill your unique purposes and potentials.

If, as explored earlier, we are truly made "in the image and likeness" of the Divine, then to "know thyself" is to know God. Working with this tradition, and especially one's personal Birth Angels, is a powerful means of discovering the purposeful love and truth of who we each uniquely are. You might even say that, just as herbalists and homeopathic practitioners understand the attributes of plants as signatures of their functions, our Birth Angels could be viewed as "signatures" of particular Divine aspects and purposes within us which are clues to who we are and what we're here to do.

To really understand this, we must be able to grasp that we are not separate from God, but that each of us is a particular Divine-Human expression of God. Thus, through the being and doing of your individual isness, you enable the Divine "I AM" to experience and expand what more it can be through, for and as *you*—with all your unique gifts, talents, capabilities, potentials and purposes. (See Appendix I, "Your Personal Birth Angels" and www.72BirthAngels.com)

(3) **Work with a specific Angelic Energy whose qualities correspond to a particular issue or challenge in your life**. We can work with the 72 Angels as "light-prescriptions" for whatever ails us, with no adverse side-effects! For example, if you are having difficulty with forgiveness, invoke the energies of HAZIEL, which supports Divine Mercy and Forgiveness. If you are dealing with the loss of a relationship or job, work with MUMIAH, the 72nd Angel that supports endings in preparation for rebirth. If you are facing a healing challenge of some kind, work with any of the several Angels, as *angles* of light, that support healing on different levels.

The five volumes of the *Book of Days* each deal with a particular aspect of our lives. Thus, if you would like guidance with a specific issue, you might want to search for a Wisdom in the volume that would relate to that. For example, if you've had an argument or difficult encounter with your partner or family member, consult Volume 4, which deals with "Relationship with Others." Read the Wisdom for the Angel that was governing during the day or time period of your encounter, or an Angel that you are spontaneously drawn to, or one with qualities that may help you to deal with the situation. Or if you're having to make an important decision about the direction of your work, consult Volume 3, "Relationship with Work and Purpose," for the Wisdoms of your own Birth Angels or any Angelic Energies that may help with the particular issues you're concerned with.

(4) **Work with both the Virtues and Inversions of the Angelic Energies.** The Kabbalah presents the 72 Angelic Energies to us with dual light-and-dark potentials as "Virtues" and "Inversions" (see the first *Birth Angels* book, 2004). Similar to psycho-therapeutic modalities that bring our inner "shadows" to light so that they might be confronted and healed, the Angels' Inversions can help to illuminate and heal our own darker feelings, attitudes and actions that may occur when our potentials and purposes are engaged inappropriately, aberrantly, and even hurtfully.

In the Angel Wisdoms of MANAKEL (the *Book of Days*), which represents "Knowledge of Good and Evil," our understandings of these two polarities are challenged as we are offered perspectives that transcend our notions of "original sin," judgment, heaven and hell. In the dual reality of the soul-body life in the physical realm, every light, or positive, aspect has a darker potential as it moves from the higher vibrations of light toward the denser vibrations of matter. Like "two sides of a coin," or "too much of a good thing," our own best traits—if misappropriated or distorted—have the potential to become our worst. The understanding we are offered is that in a cosmic paradigm in which love and light ultimately prevail, sooner or later all events and circumstances—no matter how seemingly dark—can be used for positive growth and goodness.

(5) **Do family constellation work by tapping into the Birth Angels of family members and loved ones**. Often with families and loved ones there are difficult, challenging and hurtful dynamics which are hard to understand or reconcile. By exploring the Birth Angels of all involved, you can begin to see how you have chosen, at a soul level, to come together and work with each other as opportunities for growth and transformation. Here it can be especially helpful to study not only the Virtues of each person's Birth Angels, but also their Inversions — which represent the ways in which we may negatively express when we are not acting as our true and loving selves.

This Birth Angels constellation work is especially helpful when you are not able to speak or interact with loved ones, as with those who have already departed or with whom communication at this level, or at all, is not currently possible. You can also do this same work for difficult issues with friends, colleagues and adversaries. Volume 4 of the *Book of Days*, which offers Wisdoms about relationship with others, can be especially helpful in this work.

(6) **Invoke particular Angelic Energies to discover and enhance your work/purpose.** Each of the 72 Angels have a five-day period of governing when they support our physical incarnation and life purpose. Thus, if you are beginning a project, endeavor or business, you can work not only with your own Incarnation Angel, but also with any of the Angelic Energies whose qualities correspond to your new endeavor. For example, you can invoke the first Angel VEHUIAH, who supports will and new beginnings, or if you are a

public speaker, invoke the energies of DANIEL, which amplifies the qualities of communication, eloquence and authentic expression. If you are a judge, lawyer or mediator, work with NEMAMIAH, which supports the discernment of heart-seeing, or the justice of CALIEL, which helps to balance judgment and mercy. For whatever kind of work you do, Volume 3 of the Book of Days offers Wisdoms about discovering your purpose through what you love, and then working your purpose or purposing your work so that your whole life is enlivened with the greater vitality and enthusiasm of doing what you love and loving what you do.

The 72 Angels system is being more and more utilized in healing arts and the fields of spiritual mentoring and life-coaching, astrology, color therapy, aroma essences and more. Healing arts practitioners and coaches use the 72 Angels tradition to augment their practice by working with the 72 Angels as illuminators and Divine helpers while working with clients. Invoking one of the several Angels that support healing, or the client's Birth Angels (determined by date and time of birth), the Angel of the day — or invoking a specific "angle" of Divine Light to support a particular issue — can provide insights into a client's qualities, challenges and potentials in order to bring issues to light so that deeper healing can take place. (See Appendix I for information about one's Birth Angels.)

(7) **Work with the 72 Angels to deepen your own spiritual path**. The Angelic Kabbalah is not a religion, but rather a mystical system developed by multi-traditional Kabbalists through the centuries to help people in all walks of life — regardless of creed, culture or gender — to experience direct and intimate communion with one's inner Divine.

Most spiritual and religious traditions encompass both <u>dogma</u> which includes certain beliefs and rituals, and <u>mysticism</u>, which represents personal communion and experience with the Divine. For example, the Kabbalah is the mystical heart of Judaism, Sufism the mystical aspect of Islam, and Christian mysticism has its many recognized saints, mystics and mystical events which abound in the histories of the mainstream Catholic, Protestant and Eastern traditions, as well as the more mystical, even so-called heretical sects that arose before or during formalized church doctrines, such as the Essenes, Gnostics, Cathars, Rosicrucians and others. Angels are spoken of in most of these traditions, but accounts of Angelic appearances mostly involve interactions with individuals—and they come not to convey religious "law," but the love of the Divine for the human.

The Opportunity of Change

We cannot engage in the daily art of becoming without taking on change. In Genesis 8:22 of the Bible, it is written: "While the earth remaineth, seedtime and harvest, and cold and heat, and summer and winter, and day and night shall not cease." Change is endemic—and necessary—to the ongoingness of life, and it occurs both on the inside and the outside of all life forms and throughout all aspects of creation and the natural world—though of course outer change is usually more visible. While change has shown itself to be cyclical in the historical and ongoing seasons and cycles of our planet, each cycle contains sub-cycles of gestation, new beginnings, growth, fruition, harvest and endings—and then it all starts over again, which we experience through the life passages and daily and seasonal dynamics of our own lives.

In human life, our common phrase, "people never change," is simply not true. We are changing on the outside and the inside all the time! And as we grow and the outer world changes around us, we are having to adjust continually. But inner, essential change is much more subtle, involving the relationship of our soul to both our Spirit-origin and the diverse aspects of our humanity. As the workings of our soul are broadcast into our heart, and from our heart into the rest of our parts, change may become visible by a new light that exudes from us—or in the how and why of what we do, if not the what.

This reminds me of the Zen story of the farmer who, before he was enlightened, got up in the morning, tended to the animals, worked the fields, came home for lunch, went back out to work the fields, came home for dinner, sat awhile on the porch, went to bed, and got up again. After he became enlightened, he got up in the morning, tended to the animals, worked the fields, came home for lunch, went back out to work the fields, came home for dinner, sat awhile on the porch, went to bed, and got up again. What changed for him was everything, but it was invisible to all but himself—especially to those who perceived only his actions.

The themes of change proliferate through the Angel wisdoms, especially because the Angels are here within and among us to help us receive the gifts and opportunities of outer change through the inner transformations of heart and mind and the awareness that we are not "only human," but Divine-Human beings. As change is a prime mover in our becoming, we are encouraged to be patient and loving with ourselves and each other in accepting "what is" about us or our circumstances—while we are in the process of "truing-up" our inner being with our outer expression and becoming what more we desire to be.

Imagine if we can more and more see our "same old" selves in the always-new light that the Angels do! For truly, every day we are writing a new chapter in the ongoing story of our unique lives, with moment-to-moment new possibilities of being and becoming. Every day we live in a "same but different" reality! For though we wake up every morning with ourselves, we are not exactly the same person physiologically, emotionally, mentally or spiritually that we were yesterday, or all the yesterdays before then, nor will we be at tomorrow's waking. The whole world has changed overnight—is it not likely that the ripples that go out into the world from our own being and doing are contributing to that, and vice-versa?

The transformation of the caterpillar into a butterfly is a common change metaphor for us humans. This is perhaps because the transformation of a cocooned thing into a flying thing echoes the soul cocooned within our physicality that longs for the winged, or ascendant, experiences that uproot our "feet of mortal clay" to allow us a glimpse of higher vistas.

I was once lying under some trees in a mountain forest, listening for a message that would usually come to me from the natural world whenever I was out walking. As none came, I relaxed my expectation and closed my eyes to feel the Earth under my body, the warmth of the summer sun on my face and the busy thrum of things with wings chirping and buzzing in the trees and bushes. Just then I felt a flutter on my cheek, and I opened one eye to see a beautiful butterfly doing a circular "flutter-by" of my head. My heart quickened at the beauty of its uniquely-shaped colors and sudden visitation my way. As it continued to circle my head, this came softly:

> *The butterfly flying by*
> *has no words...*
> *But if you listen to*
> *the whisper of her wings*
> *as she flutters and floats*
> *upon the light of day,*
> *you will hear all*
> *you need to know*
> *about the casting off*
> *of old forms and*
> *the lightness of beauty*
> *being freed.*

I remember wondering in the moments between taking this in and writing it down why change couldn't be this effortless-feeling—a *bearable* lightness of being. And then my mind's eye was led to the moment that a butterfly is about to emerge from its chrysalis. I realized that its wings gain the strength to fly by using them to break out of its own alchemical birthing-cocoon—just as we "earn our wings" in life by our own willingness to break through, and ultimately transform, our fears and hesitations so that we might ascend to higher ground and the sky of dreams we hold in our hearts.

The Angels tell us that it is precisely because of our "longing for sky" and our willingness to brave the shadows of our humanity to "reach up" toward the lighterness of our essential eternal being, that they are here within and among us in their Divine mission to help us do just that. And even though change is upon us in every season and moment to moment—and we continually have almost as much resistance to it as desire for it—we have been Divinely equipped to handle whatever comes our way, and to be evolved into more of the totality of who we are in the process.

The Angel Wisdoms say that it was the great desire of the I-AM Allness to know what it was which impulsed the first cosmic movement of Love, and thus change, from an unknowable "No-Thingness" unto the every-thing-and-beingness of Creation. And it is change that continues to move us and our own creations forward toward fruition, fulfillment and renewal throughout our entire lives, and beyond.

The Seasons of Our Lives

As discussed in Volume 1, the natural world is potentially our greatest teacher of life on Earth. From nature we can learn about the movements and passages of life, about being both finite form and ongoing essence, and the vital importance of relationship and interdependence for our resiliency and regeneration.

In one year nature examples an entire life cycle for living things and beings from birth, growth, maturation, blossoming and fruition to harvest, death or dormancy, gestation and rebirth. Every species of life goes through these life cycles—whether in the span of a few minutes, a few hours, years, centuries or even over the course of several millennia. What is so unique about human beings is that we have the emotional, mental, physical and spiritual faculties to contemplate and engage with the opportunities in our life cycles.

When we are young, the stages of life seem to happen so quickly from infant to toddler to child to puberty, adolescence and finally young adulthood. In a few short years we go from being utterly helpless and dependent on our family group to becoming determinedly independent and creators of our own little worlds of friendship and family. It's a really short time when you think about how our developmental faculties progress in just seven to ten years from gurgling to *googling*! And then comes our first real life gauntlet (if life or family circumstances haven't already challenged us), when hormones kick us into adolescence and our physiology starts to rage, often before we have the mental and emotional maturity to handle it. And all this while we are trying to emancipate at least a little bit from our parents so that we can individuate—while at the same time trying to find a place of belonging with our peers.

These years, from the ground zero of birth to around 18, can be the most difficult in our lives because, in general, we lack the consciousness to understand what's going on within us. We are extremely sensitive in our young years, more than we know, and everything affects us and gets stored within us—sometimes not to be dealt with for many years. But as we advance into adulthood—with more awareness, more conscious relationships, life purposing, work and general life experience—we begin to think about life in the past, present and future, and what we want to give to and receive from it.

This is the point at which the road of life forks for many of us, and when we choose either consciously or unconsciously, to chase quantity or quality of life. But I think most of us seek the "middle road," where both is possible. A life in which we can achieve our goals and dreams and take in "all life has to offer," while also becoming more aware and engaging of self and others and the meanings that underlie our actions and activities—and particularly the meaning and purpose of our own existence.

It takes a lot of courage to be a human being—to have our soul-light encased and even forgotten in the thick slowness of matter. And to go through long periods of not knowing how to, or even that we can, access the eternal on tap within us as we are being buffeted about by the vagaries of time, the winds of change and the storms of life, love and longing.

And so, for all this, the 72 Angels tradition says that the Divine accompanies us throughout the seasons of our lives as *angles* of Its own light—not only watching over us, but dwelling within us to help us access the Divinity within, and as, the essence of our humanity. In our communions and co-creativities with the 72 Angels, we are awakened into awareness of our love-and-truth nature. Our soul-light which animates and ennobles our humanity is amplified, and we are shown the lifelines of heart and soul within us that give us continual access to "Spirit"—the eternal greater Divine from which our soul originates and which also dwells within us, as us.

It is said that the Angels are a gift to us from the Divine Heart. If we allow ourselves to receive this endless unconditional love of the Divine, we can learn to love and have compassion and understanding for ourselves. Once we have this Divinely-born self-love and compassion, it is easy to extend them to others—and in so doing always have what we need for ourselves, and more, from both Heaven and Earth.

It seems fitting that the Angels would work with us in connection to the cycles of the natural world. As those who work with the deeper presences of nature tell us, all manner of flora and fauna are watched over by and in communion with spirits, devas and angels. How natural, then, that we too should have our Angelic allies, as aspects of the Divine attending us through all our days, and as emissaries and amplifiers of the eternal in all the seasons and cycles of our lifetime.

Just as with the Divine and the entire cosmos since the first "moments" of Emanation and differentiation of the One into the many of Creation, everything and everyone is birthed, lives and moves forward through cycles of ebb and flow in the context of **relationship**. Thus, in the first cycle of 72 messages starting March 21, there is a focus on what the soul regards as its origin and primary relationship, which is with the Divine Itself. It is our soul's cosmic birth from which all else emerges: relationship with self, our life meaning and purpose, our loved ones and those in our close circles, and finally the world at large.

And so, the 72 Angels in their daily support cycle five times a year (72 x 5 + some overlapping days = 365), through the seasons of our year in relationship with the different aspects of our lives, with each year as a season in our life, and our life a season of the Divine on Earth.

Spring ~ 3/21–6/2: Relationship with the Divine. The newborn green of Spring symbolizes our cosmic birth and what the soul regards as our primary relationship with the Divine Itself as our origin. Just as with the Spring rebirth of so many forms of Creation in the natural world, we too experience the quickening of new beingness and reawakening to the world in fresh ways as we sprout new beginnings and creations that have been gestating within us during the Winter.

Summer ~ 6/3–8/16: Relationship with Self. This is a time of exploration and celebration of ourselves through self-love, gladness, the lighterness of being, living, loving and playing in the flowering and ripening of our unique potentials. This is our most impactful relationship during our time on Earth, because who we are with and within ourselves affects *how* we are with all others.

Fall ~ 8/17–10/29: <u>Relationship with Work and Purpose.</u> This is the season for harvesting the fruits of our summer and then scattering new seeds as we get back to work after vacations and times of fun and relaxation. While outer forms begin to fall away, we bring focus to our activities and become more purposeful as we continue our individuation through new ideas, projects and collaborations, and perhaps a new job, recommitment to our work or a new school year.

The "Holy-days" of Late Fall/Early Winter ~ 10/30–1/8: <u>Relationship with Others.</u> Here the Angels encourage heartfulness in our interpersonal relatings at the time of year when we gather with loved ones and those in our immediate circles to celebrate the holidays and holy days of the season. In coming together with those who matter most, where the need for forgiveness and healing is often most apparent, we see the opportunity through self-transformation to transform and re-enliven our relationships.

Winter ~ 1/9–3/20: <u>Relationship with Community and the World.</u> With Volume 5, the five Angelic cycles of the year come to a close. Here the Daily Wisdoms invite us into the darker inwardness of winter in contemplation of self and purpose and how we might bring more of who we are and what we value to our communities, the collective consciousness and our relationship with the Earth. Just as with the dormant seeds buried in the dark soil of winter, our own most profound growth occurs in the deeper humus of heart and soul. From the gestation and nurturing of our own withins, new ideas, wisdoms and ways are formed and made ready to sprout a renewed and even reborn self unto the soon-awakening world of Spring.

As mentioned in Volume 1, the seasonal references would be reversed for the southern hemisphere, and less dramatic for those who live closer to the equator. My suggestion is to engage with the *Book of Days* as per the date, and apply the seasonal references as metaphors to the personal dynamics of your life that are always moving through cycles of ebb and flow, waxing and waning, gestation and renewal.

42

The Angelic Flowering of Summer

Summer is the time of year when our senses are infused with a multitude of intoxicating scents and sounds. The musky sensuality of the heated earth, the moist green of cut grass and the sudden perfume of flowers and their aromatic rainbows of color, the constant day and evening medley of bees, birds, crickets and other insects. Days drenched in sunlight and warm evening breezes wafting on bared skin are a constant invitation to lightness of being, self-blossoming and enjoyment. In the Summer, we are urged "to dive into the deep end of a pool [with] a courage you don't have the rest of the year... grateful and easy, with no eyes on you, and no past. Summer just opens the door and lets you out." (Deb Caletti - *Honey, Baby, Sweetheart*)

Summer is when we most display and share the beauties of ourselves with each other in play and relaxation, easy connections with friends and loved ones and spontaneous or anticipated adventures. Summer, more than any other season, is a time when it is so much easier to be in the isness of ourselves and life and to revel in the flow of now and relax our concerns about the past and the future. Here and now, in this lighterness of being, the Angels of Summer love to support us in the stream of our natural flow and the sensory self-awareness and enjoyment that Summer invites.

The Daily Wisdoms
The 72 Angels' Days of Heart Influence

As a reminder, each Daily Wisdom corresponds to the day's Angel when it is in its "heart dominion," and thus expressing its particular qualities of Divine Love and Truth through the quickening of these in our own heart, and from there into all our parts. By checking in with the Daily Wisdom at the beginning of our day, our awareness is awakened, and we are lovingly prompted to take our hearts with us when we walk out our door into the world!

In case you did not start the *Book of Days* series with Volume 1, repeated here are the various associations to the daily Angel wisdoms which relate to the Angel's position on the Tree of Life and give clues to its nature: the Sephira of the Tree in which the Angel resides, its overlighting Archangel, astrological and date associations and more.

Sephirot Pages: These introduce each of the Nine Sephirot (vessel or sphere) in which each order, or choir, of eight Angels resides on the Tree of Life, as well as the qualities and functions of their overlighting Archangel. The Tenth Sephira, MALKUTH, is related to the manifestation of Earth and represents the realm of "Ascended Souls," so there are no Angels assigned to this Sephira in the Tree of Life symbology (except the Archangels).

Dates of the Angel's Heart-Influence: The current day of the Angel's expression and support through our heart plane is bolded; the other dates represent its four other "heart-days" during the year. Since it is helpful to be aware of your Heart Angel not only on your birthday, but also its other four days of influence, you may want to mark your personal calendar with all five days. Note also that the yearly cycle for the 72 Angels begins March 21, the time of the Spring Equinox, which is the beginning of "Nissan," the first month of the year in the Jewish calendar. In my research I also ran across an obscure variant in the date attributions of the Angelic cycles, but the one used in all the *Birth Angels* materials is the cycle that the 12th-15th century school of Isaac the Blind and his followers and fellow

Kabbalists were working with throughout the centuries, including Kabaleb in the 20ᵗʰ century. (See Appendix II in Volume I)

An Angel's full day of influence goes from 12:00 am midnight to 12:00 am midnight, 24 hours later (00:00-24:00 in Europe, etc.). A few of the Angels' days overlap to support a total of 365 days. In a leap year of 366 days, the Angel for February 28 also governs the 29ᵗʰ. The "a.m." designation always goes from 12:00 a.m. midnight to 12:00 p.m. noon (00:00-12), and the "p.m." from 12:00 p.m. noon to 12:00 a.m. midnight (12:00-24:00). Of course, 12:00 a.m. is a cusp minute for both day and night. An Angel that governs for a day and a half, for example, 4/16 + 17 am, would span from 12:00 a.m. midnight as the 15ᵗʰ passes to the 16ᵗʰ, to 12:00 p.m. noon on the 17ᵗʰ (midnight to midnight to noon) (00:00-24:00-12:00).

Note: Kabbalists have historically worked with the 72 Angels through their correspondences to the Zodiacal degrees totaling 360, the circumference of a circle—which Isaac Newton noted was likely because many ancient civilizations marked time with a 360-day lunar calendar. Ultimately a correspondence of degrees to actual days was needed in order to accommodate our 365-day calendar, which meant that a few of the Angelic Energies would be attributed to more than one day (see Appendix I). Because the degrees to days correspondences change slightly every year, it can be helpful to be aware of the Angelic Energy that comes before and after each of your Birth Angels or the one you are working with at a particular date or time, and notice if you feel more resonance with one than another. (Thanks to Tristan Llop, son of esoteric astrologer and author Enrique Llop, writing as Kabaleb, for explaining this to me!)

Ultimately our lives are about what we do with the energies that are presented to us—for we have the innate power to use everything that comes our way as an ally and catalyst for growth.

The Angel's number and name: The number for each Angel represents the order of its position on the Tree of Life and its degrees of correspondence to the Zodiacal wheel of time—and if you study astrology and numerology these may give additional insight into both the Angels and the stars. The Angel's name is a transliteration of its Hebrew name. The origin of the 72 names is what the Kabbalah refers to as the 72 "Intelligences" or "Names of God" as the "Shem HaMephorash,"), which are each composed of a three-letter combination derived from a "decoding" of Exodus 14:19-21 in Hebrew. While vowels were originally left out of the Angels' Hebrew Names to create ambiguity in order to protect the sacred Names of God, in later centuries the "niqqud" (vowel marks) were added to help with pronunciation. Each Angel's name in transliteration ends in either "IAH" or "EL," denoting that the name is a Name and Quality of God. Some Kabbalah literature says that IAH represents the feminine aspect and EL the masculine, representing the inherent masculine-feminine unity within the Divine which is expressed in duality as polarities, as with all manifestations in life.

You will notice if you consult other sources through the ages that the spellings of the Angels' names vary greatly. This is the result of varied dialects and permutations in the Hebrew language and its transliterations through centuries of dispersion of the Jewish people into different cultures and sects. Thus, the varied spellings you may encounter are not necessarily wrong, just different. I have done extensive research on this, but in the end have chosen to follow in my own work most of the spellings that the works of Kabaleb put forth based on his extensive research of prominent medieval and Renaissance Kabbalists working with this system.

Pronunciation guide: This is given to help with saying or chanting the Angel's name aloud in meditation or prayer as you invite the Angel's energies to expand within you. All the names are emphasized (shown in ALL CAPS) on the last syllable, IAH or EL, to show that the name is a quality and aspect of God. Names with more than two syllables have two accented syllables, as in "Neh-MA-mee-YAH." Kabbalah creation cosmology regards the sounds and forms of the Hebrew letters as having the power to transmit Divine Energies and even bring forth new life. This is akin to the use of the word "Om" and Sanskrit chants to invoke the Divine within.

Angel's quality/function and G/R/S designation: This represents the Divine attribute which the Angel embodies and amplifies within you, and whether the attribute is expressed outwardly (G, for "Going out" from the Divine and down the Tree of

Life toward manifestation), inwardly (R for "Returning" back up the Tree to the Divine through ascending consciousness), or in a state of equilibrium which can be expressed either outwardly or inwardly (S for Stabilized).

As discussed in the section "Our Personal Birth Angels," the qualities of the Angels seem to have been attributed beyond the literal meanings of their Hebrew letters to reflect in part their astrological, Archangelic and other Tree of Life associations according to medieval astrologers working within the Kabbalah and the 72 Angels tradition.

Keynote phrase: This is a short by-line I have been inspired to add to capture the essence of the Angel's function.

Overlighting Archangel: This is the Archangel that governs the Sephira which the Angel resides within on the Tree of Life, and whose qualities overlight or influence the functions of the eight Angels in that Sephira and the Angelic order (choir) that the Angels belong to. There are eight Angels in each of the Nine (out of Ten) Sephirot on the Tree (8x9=72). Because so many people working with Angels in our modern world seem to be working with the Archangel energies, it is perhaps interesting to note that throughout the world's Angelic traditions and the ancient wisdoms, Archangels' were seen as the guardians of lands, nations and societal groups; whereas the Angels are said to be attendant to individuals because their vibrations are nearer to life forms. However, until this tradition was revived in the 1980's-90's by the work of Kabaleb (first published under his friend Haziel's name), only a few of the Angels' individual names have been commonly known to Angel enthusiasts.

The Angel's sign, planet and 5-day period of "Incarnation" influence: Each Angel's astrological correspond-dences relate to its five consecutive days of influence once a year on the Incarnation, or physical, plane, which also corresponds to 5 degrees of the Zodiac (72x5=360)—taking into consideration the adjustments made for a 365-day year (see Appendix I). If you are interested in astrology, this can help to shed additional light on the Angel's qualities. (Neptune and Uranus were added later when they were discovered.) Although the Angels in their Incarnation influence (physicality, will and life purpose) are not the focus of the *Book of*

48

Days, I included the dates of each Angel's Incarnation influence (the date spread next to the sign/planet) for ease in discovering your Incarnation Angel—which would be the one supporting the five-day span that corresponds to the five-days around your birth.

For example, if your birthday is March 20, your Incarnation Angel would be #72 MUMIAH, which governs March 16-20. Again, however, because of the yearly fluctuation of degrees correspondent to days, if your birthday is the first or last day or the Angel's date-span of support, then it is suggested to check the Angel closest to yours, being the previous or next, whichever applies—and notice which is more resonant. (See also Appendix I for a complete list of the 72 Angels with their corresponding 5-day span of Incarnation influence, as well as the 20-minute period during the 24-hour day when they support our intellect.)

"I AM THAT WHICH...:" Here the Angel introduces itself as a particularized aspect (**"that which"**) of the One "I AM" which is its purpose to amplify in our human lives—thus helping us to fulfill the unique "I Am that which" that each of us are as a particular constellation and expression of Divine-Human qualities.

The Angel's message: As detailed above, all 72 Angels cycle for at least one day five times a year, effectively taking us through the seasons of the year and of our lives. Since everything and everyone exists in the context of relationship, the first cycle of 72 messages starting March 21 starts with the new birth of the natural world which also symbolizes the soul's cosmic birth and relationship to the Divine. From there we move into the four subsequent cycles—our relationship with self, work and purpose, others in our close circles, and then to our communities and the world at large. Thus, all five cycles comprise a journey in one year through all the literal and symbolic themes and seasons of our lives.

The Angels seem to have different tones in their "speech" at different times—some are lighter, some more serious, some "teacherly" and others passionate—but all consistently loving and inclusive. Also, sometimes they speak as "I" and sometimes as "we." I continue to sense that in their roles as differentiated expressions of the Divine Oneness, "I" and "we" are interchangeable for them.

The light-thread that is woven through all the different messages is about <u>the power of love to reveal and expand the truth of who we are and what we are here to be and do for ourselves, each other and the Divine Itself within and as each of us.</u>

The "Amen" at the end of each Wisdom. I realized I had been hearing "Amen" at the end of each Wisdom from the beginning of the *Book of Days* and had not been fully conscious of it until working on the third volume—and so in subsequent revised editions I have inserted it throughout. Researching the origins of Amen confirms the usual Hebrew and Christian use of Amen as "so be it" at the end of prayers. In addition, Amen encompasses the Hebrew letters "aleph-mem-nun" (confirmed, reliable, have faith, believe), which also correspond to the word "emuna" (faith) and "emet" (truth). There are also associations with the Egyptian god Amun (also Amen, the creator of all things, king of the gods) and the Hindu Sanskrit word Aum (or Om, the Absolute, Omnipresent, Manifest and Unmanifest).

In Hebrew, "Amen" is a word of power, a kind of cosmic "abracadabra" to activate and transmit the energy of the Divine within us and to call us back to our hearts from wherever else we are. And so here, as "Amen...," the three dots are meant to extend a loving and compassionate space to do that.

The Daily "Heart Angel." Remember, again, that the Daily Wisdoms are given as messages from the 72 Angels when they are in their "heart dominion." Thus, in their daily roles as "Heart Angels," they support us throughout our day with their particular qualities of Divine Love and Truth in order to help cultivate our ability to draw from our heart's infinite resources of soul and Spirit. Thus may we ennoble our lives with the cultivation of self-love and love of others, compassion, understanding, forgiveness, intuition, soul-truth, wisdom and the greater reality of the eternal.

And so now, may you continue your daily heart-journey with the 72 Angels with joy, love and the flowering of summer in your heart, mind, body and soul!

June 3—10

Angels 1—8

Sephira 1

KETHER ~ Crown/Will

Overlighting Archangel

METATRON ~ "Angel of the Presence"
"King of the Angels," representing unmanifested
enlightenment and the connection of Light between
Divine energy and human spiritual energy
(Related to the prophet Enoch & Akashic Records)

---

1 **VEHUIAH**

2 **JELIEL**

3 **SITAEL**

4 **ELEMIAH**

5 **MAHASIAH**

6 **LELAHEL**

7 **ACHAIAH**

8 **CAHETEL**

Soar
into the sky
of your heart
with every
new dawn,
knowing
that the
lighter
you become,
the higher
you will
fly.

1 VEHUIAH

(vay-HOO-ee-YAH)
Will and New Beginnings (G)
'One who begins again and again'
Archangel ~ METATRON
Aries / Uranus (3/21-25)

I AM THAT WHICH...

energizes and lightens you with the reminder that today is always, as you say, 'the first day of the rest of your life,' so that you might use the endings of yesterday to propel you into new beginnings.

Every new today can bring you the energy and fresh insight to carry forward the gifts of yesterday and let go of the rest, if you will. You have the capacity to soar in the sky of your heart with every new dawn—and the lighter you become, the higher you can fly. So let go and keep letting go, as there is always more ahead to partake of— more life, more love, more to create from the soul, heart, mind and belly of you! Let every new step start from your heart, and the rest of your parts will 'play their part' to help make the way ahead with the whole of you.

Remember that relationship with yourself as a Divine-Human being is reflective of relationship with your inner Divine and the humus, or earthenness, of your being. Do you give the heart and soul that animates your humanity a voice in your life doings and decisions? Do you rest when your body tells you it's tired, and give your body water and nourishment when it is thirsty and hungry? Just as with plants in your home or garden, do you honor and care for the garden of your own multi-part being with your true needs and desires, potentials and purposes?

Despite all life-affirming intentions, it is easy for the demands of life to become like chokeweeds that diminish and deplete the

53

nutrients and conditions needed for your own healthy growth. And therefore, while you may be focused on responsibilities and challenges, dreams or delights, remember that being is just as important as doing. Because wherever and however you are in any present moment will likely determine the quality of your next moment—and your future experiences.

If you utilize the Divine within your own heart and soul as your personal 'spiritual navigation system,' you will treasure the journeys in your life as much as any of your destinations. Often your beginning journeys have much momentum and vision to let you know you're on the right road, and then the challenges show up. But every meandering mile, detour and delay, every bend or obstacle in the road, is an opportunity for you to discover not only more of your outer world, but especially more of your inner and 'other-worlds' which can give you strength, stamina and extra 'throttle' just when you need it! And with your inner Divine as guide and compass, you will have both time and timelessness to partake of the magical experiences and learning opportunities that unexpected happenings and serendipitous encounters offer.

I, VEHUIAH, am the Angelic light-beckoner of the Divine within you that urges you toward all the new and wonderful people, events and opportunities that continually enliven your life and bring more of your totality into expression. Always, dear beloved, when you are willing to start anew, endings will be the fodder for wisdom-making and the fire for new beginnings. So may it be! Amen...

3/22 * **6/4** * 8/18 + 19am * 10/31 * 1/10

2 JELIEL

(YAY-lee-EL)
Love and Wisdom (G)
'One who uses love to make wisdom'
Archangel ~ METATRON
Aries / Saturn (3/26-30)

I AM THAT WHICH...

helps you to embrace the worthiness of your own being and to cultivate self-love and wisdom for living in a way that is true to you and which impacts how you will love and inspire others.

When you look at a flower, do you not love it for its surprising and unique beauty and marvel at the perfection of its sheer isness? Do you wish it were a different flower, more like some other flower? Of course not! You are as unique as that flower, here to blossom with all the colors of your own rainbow and to harvest the fruit of your own creativity. For just like every petal of every flower, all your parts and your greater totality are unparalleled in the universe. The hues in your 'hue-man' beingness cannot be replicated by any other, and we of the Angelic realms marvel at the wonders of you!

Just as in the first differentiation of the Divine Oneness into Everything, everything you experience, create and offer in life begins with the self, as one, and radiates out to the many. Love yourself and know that you ARE Love in both 'noun' and 'verb!'—for the dynamics in all your relatings are affected by relationship with yourself. If you harbor shame, guilt or unworthiness, your secret self-judgment will be projected outwardly as judgment and intolerance of others. And if you do not love yourself, not only will it compromise your ability to truly love others, but it may be uncomfortable, even painful, for others to love you because their love will not have a welcome resting place within you.

55

Loving yourself—the whole of yourself—is not a selfish thing—it is necessary in order to live truly and rightly in your world and to bring forth loving creations and relationships. The key is in knowing and feeling yourself as a unique expression of the Divine Self and Its desire to experience life and love through you in the ways only you can. There is no question of your worthiness when you understand that your true lineage is of the Divine Itself. 'The apple does not fall far from the tree' because the apple contains the seed of the tree within it. And so, just as you are loved by That Which created you, love and care for yourself and your own creations.

As for wisdom, you cannot achieve wisdom without love, because it is love which expands and gives meaning to all your knowledge and experience. Wisdom results as an alchemy of the heart and must be forged in this innermost cauldron into which all your being and doing are commingled with your intuition, feeling and the direct knowing of soul that is broadcast to your heart. Together these create a life-giving elixir that imparts to you the secrets of life and guides you toward becoming a fully realized Divine-Human being.

I, JELIEL, am the fire of Divine Love that commingles with your own soul-light and draws you within to be purified and illuminated. Love yourself, and you will be loving the Divine within as we love you. Love yourself, and you will draw others who will love you. Love yourself, and you will inspire others to love their own beautiful beings as well. Love yourself, and that love will be imparted through all you create.

Ask any question, seek any purpose, and the answer will be the same: Love, and the heart-truth that love reveals, which is that you were conceived and made of love and it is love that grows the truth of who you are. This is the wisdom and the mystery of life. Amen...

3 SITAEL

(SIT-ah-EL)
Construction of Worlds (G)
'One who loves creations into being'
Archangel ~ METATRON
Aries / Jupiter (3/31-4/4)

I AM THAT WHICH...

*illuminates the blueprint of the Divine Architect at work within you
to help you use harmonious thought and feeling 'substructures' in
order to accomplish noble endeavors and works.*

*Whatever you set out to build, let the cornerstones be forged in
the creative fires of your heart so that the foundation will be strong
enough to support the whole, yet flexible enough to withstand winds
of change and shifting sands. Then the inner spaces will have the
grounding to support inspiration and the co-creation of dreams,
plans and good works. Thus, if you discover a crack in your
foundation, look to the deeper interior aspects to find where there is
a disturbance or dysfunction in thought or perception. Re-examine
your core values, what matters most, what you love, what is true,
and that which supports the parts as well as the whole of you. In at
least one of these will be a factor that is causing stress on the whole.*

*We speak of you as Divine-Human beings, and we could also say
that you are divinely human, or humanly divine. But the whole truth
is that all you are is of the Divine, for there is nothing that is not.
Therefore, the physical matter of your 'flesh and bone' is not less
Divine—just denser vibrations of Divine energy. It is the denser
vibrations of form and structure that physically support the lighter
ephemeral vibrations of your being, giving your Divine soul-essence
a vehicle for manifestation and the means to 'go forth and multiply'
variations of your unique potential. And simultaneously, even*

57

symbiotically, it is that inner ephemeral substance that gives your physical being a reason and purpose for being.

With the birth of Creation was born otherness into the physicality of time and place, mirroring again and again the eternal 'moment' that One became two, which brought forth a third and fourth, into ongoing creations. Just as you, and all, are thus diverse expressions of what was once hidden in Divine Oneness—your own creations reveal feelings, thoughts, ideas and possibilities within you cannot find fulfillment until they take form.

Dear divinely human creator-builder, may you draw from my light as SITAEL to see that every thought, feeling and idea you hold within you projects out into the world of form to create its own world. Thus, use your creations to better know and grow the love and truth of who you are, that both you and your creations may soar in the sky of endless possibility held within all your imaginings, with the power to positively impact your fellow beings. And we suggest to always remember — what you build or do not build for yourself, you are also building or not building for the world. Amen...

4 ELEMIAH

(eh-LEH-mee-YAH)
Divine Power (G)
'One who implants the tree of life within'
Archangel ~ METATRON
Aries / Mars (4/5-9)

I AM THAT WHICH...

helps you to draw upon the energies of the natural world to support your own inner resources, strengthen your resiliency and sustain your life-cycles.

Your human nature has a close and deep kinship with the natural world, for you are made from the commingling of earth and the spirit that enlivens your earthen substance—and thus you are supported by both. Just as in the natural world, the physical humus of your nature needs food, moisture, light, air and other life-force elements and energies for nourishment, growth, blossoming, fruition and re-seeding. The Divine—the great 'gardener' of life—supplies these to the things and beings of the natural world through the richness of diversity and abundant, ever-evolving life cycles—which in turn supply you with a bounty of light, water, food, oxygen and shelter. But nature has another more mysterious gift for you—a deep sentient intelligence which feels you, knows what you need and reacts to what you do and desire. This pervasive intelligence of the natural world is the host and co-creator of your world, and the greatest ally of your physical beingness.

Just as with your own nature, the natural world blossoms in the presence of love and nurturing, and tends to wither or resist around neglectful, disruptive or polluting energies. Thus, if you want to access and collaborate with the intelligent, creative power of the

59

natural world, you must approach with heart and the willingness to feel, listen and receive.

Nature teaches all you need to know about the gifts of resiliency, shelter and interdependence that living things and creatures can offer to each other. From nature you can learn how to be connected with others and yet leave enough space so that you have room to grow and accommodate each other's need for light and shade, openness and shelter, independence and interdependence. She can show you how to bend in a storm, weather the winds of change, and withstand, as well as thrive, through the seasons of life. She will teach you how to revel in your fullness and recover from your losses...how to balance too much and not enough...and to understand that your strength as a whole lies in the strength, diversity and interdependence of your parts, individually and in togetherness. For each adds something unique to the soil and soul of your own being as well as to the 'soul of the world,' as each being in nature adds to the regenerative chain of life that nurtures and provides for all.

I, ELEMIAH, am the emanated expression of the elemental light-powers of the Divine. Thus I offer you these that I AM as the fire of a purifying truth, the waters of a cleansing love, the earthen matter that gives your soul grounding, and the breath of life-force within you that continues to breathe you forth into the wonders of being. You are a sustainable and regenerative source and resource in the creations of time. We of the Divine cherish our part in the beautiful flowering of your life, and we revel in the unique hues of love and truth that you unfold in the commingled light of your Divine-Human beingness.

Thus may you go forth to glorify and proliferate by bringing forth the generative light-power of the Divine in all you imagine and all you do in your time and timelessness upon your Earth. Amen...

5 MAHASIAH

(mah-HAH-see-YAH)
Rectification (G)
'One who returns to what is true for love's sake'
Archangel ~ METATRON
Aries / Sun (4/10-14)

I AM THAT WHICH...

helps to free you from the fear of so-called mistakes by understanding the nature of life as a push and pull between chaos and order, instability and balance, thrust and course-correction in order to continually create new life and possibilities.

As nature has exampled and the wise among you have mused, if you want to partake of the fruits of life, you must be willing to go out on some limbs. 'Mistakes' reflect the variety of ways a thing may be done or undone. Like the many 'takes' it can require to get a scene just right for a film, so do the scenarios of your life sometimes need many and varied takes. And thus a 'mis-take' is just your cue to take it again! So please dear one, while you are empowered by acknowledging the need for rectification, do not let it harden into a tyranny of self-judgment. Your life provides you the breathing room for continual course-correcting. Imagine driving down the road and you look away for a moment, only to look back and see that you are about to drive into oncoming traffic. If you began to berate and demean yourself for looking away, instead of instinctively correcting your trajectory—you might not be here to read the rest of this message! That is how derailing and dangerous self-judgment can be—usually much moreso than the seeming mistake itself.

May our Angelic Divine light within you help you to not only learn from your experiences and illuminate a course of rectification when needed, but also give you the deeper-seeing at times to straighten or correct what is about to 'go crooked' before it happens. This may come through dreams, intuitions, coincidental encounters or conversations, or the sudden hesitations or forethoughts that may occur just before you embark upon a course of action or say or do something you 'won't be able to take back.' Your willingness to heed the signs and subtle communications in your life will give you that magical feeling that you are being watched over and collaborated with not only from without, but from within by a Presence that knows and cares for you deeply and personally.

The more you rely on this inner Presence, the way forward will become less winding and more direct, and you will become more conscious and trusting of dynamics occurring on several levels at once within and around you. It will feel as if you and your inner guides and supporters are in continual conversation and co-creation. And indeed we are—for you are never alone in your life journey!

In summary, dear one, use my MAHASIAH light, commingled with your own soul-light, to create more of who you truly are—rather than focusing on what you are not. There is no such thing as failure, only the willingness to keep learning. And so be willing for love's sake to 'take it again,' realizing and allowing that what is true for you will likely change and grow into new truths as your feet continue to follow your heart.

So may it lovingly and truly be for you. Amen...

6 LELAHEL

(LAY-lah-HEL)
Light of Understanding (G)
'One who transforms knowledge into illumination"
Archangel ~ METATRON
Aries / Venus (4/15-20)

I AM THAT WHICH...

helps you to seek knowledge based on what is truly relevant for your life and to deepen understanding of yourself and your purposes through self-acceptance, love, and the truths of your heart.

We want you to know that even while you are caught up in the things of your world, especially concerns of the past and the future, whatever you want to know and understand is available to you where our world and yours meet—in your heart. Here in the eternal now-here of your heart, the individual one meets the Source One and the desire to know meets All-knowing. Here in your heart you are able to receive truths for your life—but always with this caveat: the truths given will be relative—meaning that part of truth's wholeness which is relevant to you, your needs, desires and the workings of your particular purposes—calibrated to what you are able and willing to receive at the time, even as in this sharing. Truths come through you as thoughts, feelings, intuitions, a sudden dawning of awareness, dreams, synchronicities and uncanny correspondences of events, encounters and conversations. That said, there will be hues of some truths given that will be as germinating light-seeds in the humus of your being until your inner soil and season are ready for the flowering of understanding.

For all the inner and outer journeys you will take throughout the course of your life, I, LELAHEL, promise you this: even if you do not feel us at times, you take every small or grand step and every fearful or courageous journey in the company of the Angelic Divine—we who are the many light-qualities of the Divine at vibrational levels that enable you to receive us. And we devote our eternal efforts to you in time that you might understand this while you are still in your Earth-life:

You are not ever 'only human,' but a spark of the Divine housed in a particularity of form that gives your soul a unique expression and 'leg to stand on' in physical life. If you would truly know and *feel* this—that you (and each) are a unique Divine-Human constellation of qualities here to express the commingled wonders of Heaven and Earth in ways that only you in your particular multi-faceted beingness can—it would change everything for you. Everything for all. Everything. May this understanding take root and grow in you, that your light may ever increase.

So may it be. Amen...

7 ACHAIAH

(ah-KAH-hee-YAH)
Patience (G)
'One who brings the stillness'
Archangel ~ METATRON
Taurus / Mercury (4/21-25)

I AM THAT WHICH...

helps you to cultivate patience and inner stillness with your strivings and stumblings, your growing and becoming, in order to let events unfold for the better understanding of your purpose among them.

In your world you can become quickly impatient with not knowing, not doing or having, and waiting for something to happen. Each life is a choreography of meeting and departing energies at a grand ball of dances at different tempos and time signatures. Sometimes it is a fast dance, and sometimes a slow one. And as you are not the only one dancing (since your fellow beings are dancing with and around you, and so are we), sometimes you must wait upon your dance partners and the fluctuating rhythms of diverse 'life-songs' to synchronize the next steps. And sometimes you must wait upon your own readiness, or for time itself to 'play your song.'

If you can fathom that the unseen is just as much a partner in the workings of your world as the visible, would this help you to be more patient when you are not seeing, being or having what you want in the immediate? With endless patience even for your impatience, we hope so! Your inner atmosphere of patience is the opportunity for you to experience the sacred in-between moments— the pause between breath in and out, between two notes, the fertile silence between what is said and what is not yet spoken, and the micro-seconds between the beats of your own heart. Here in the in-between shimmers the eternal, where you have all the time and timelessness you might ever want or need for the blossoming of potential.

I, ACHAIAH, assure you dear oft-impatient one, that the patience which cultivates presence, self-love and compassion is one of the greatest gifts you can give to your whole self. Howevermuch your soul, or your ego, may desire your acceleration of wisdom and understanding, success of one kind or another, or just getting 'from here to there,' you will come to these in the true and right time for all parts of you in tandem—heart, mind, body and soul. In this way no part of you shall be left behind that might ultimately weaken the whole.

When you become impatient with any part of yourself, hold that part in compassion and tenderness as you would your child who is still riding a bicycle with training wheels. Allowing yourself that space without judgment or impatience will enable you to make a quantum leap from where you are to where you want to be. We see it happen just like that all the time in both time and eternity!

So dear one, be in the flow of your life and let time unfold you as we keep the eternal flame of your soul strong with our Angelic light. Amen...

3/28 * **6/10** * 8/25 * 11/6 * 1/16

8 CAHETEL

(KAH-heh-TEL)
Divine Blessings (G)
'One who conducts the flow of plenty'
Archangel ~ METATRON
Taurus / Moon (4/26-30)

I AM THAT WHICH...

helps you to recognize the blessings of your unique life, whatever your circumstances, and to access your inner Divine Design for fulfillment and plenty through endeavors that are in alignment with the truths of both your body-mind and heart-soul.

You can lose sight of your blessings when you have forgotten what matters most to you or when your mind is full of things you don't have that you want or think you 'should' have. One of the secrets to increasing your blessings is not just the thought of gratitude, but the <u>feeling</u> of it. So before we address any ideas or feelings of lack you may be nursing, and ways to heal that sense of lack, we ask you to take a few moments to make a list of the blessings that are in your life. As you write down each one, let that feeling of gratitude come into your heart—for what you already have and for whatever the universe will continue to bring you in one form or another that belongs to be with you. For the times when you feel only lack or misfortune, we say this: <u>You are either courageously choosing lack from a soul level in order to heal and evolve certain aspects of yourself, or you are broadcasting mixed signals into life about what you truly want.</u>

In terms of choosing lack, your soul knows that the opportunity in lack is to create a trigger for those feelings such as fear, vulnerability and desperation to come to the surface so that they can be healed. Each time you heal something as an individual, everyone

67

around you is positively affected. Sometimes even whole groups of souls incarnate in the context of lack to bring awareness, compassion and healing to not only themselves, but other groups as well. When you realize that you are here to explore and express your uniqueness, seeming lack and other 'negative' or contracted conditions in your life can be used as contrast and impetus to bring more of your potential into being.

In terms of sending mixed signals, it is human nature for the different parts of you to want different things. Ideally your varied desires complement each other for the benefit of your whole being. However, for example, your heart and mind each have their own diverse appetites and sometimes pursue desires that may undermine each other. The disparity of desires can create inner conflict and impedance in the energy flow that naturally attracts what you desire at the deepest and truest levels of your being. In addition, one of the greatest underminers of plenty is when what you desire is continually at odds with what you believe to be possible for you.

Thus, your greater challenge is not so much getting what you want (we always help with that)—but rather knowing clearly what it is you want in a way that includes heart/soul and mind/body believing wholeheartedly that what you want is possible, and feeling that it is true and right for you to have it. We cannot determine that for you, and it's not a matter of what you should want or do. Only you can discover what you truly want and come into harmony, as well as commitment and trust, within yourself about it.

And so, dear one, I, CAHETEL, say to you: let all your parts be in accord to draw forth what your heart and soul desire. Be in a state of gladness knowing that what you want also wants you, and is on its way to you because of your unconflicted feeling and desire for it.

And finally, invite us to expand our Angelic light within you to help you rejoice in your blessed life and to feel the infinite flow always within you and you within it. Amen...

June 11—June 19

Angels 9—16

Sephira 2

CHOKMAH ~ Wisdom

Overlighting Archangel

RAZIEL ~ 'Secrets of God'
Spiritual guidance, keeper of wisdom
and revealer of the mysteries

---

9 HAZIEL

10 ALADIAH

11 LAUVIAH

12 HAHAIAH

13 YEZALEL

14 MEBAHEL

15 HARIEL

16 HAKAMIAH

9 HAZIEL

(HAH-zee-EL)
Divine Mercy and Forgiveness (S)
'One who sees with the light of love'
Archangel ~ RAZIEL
Taurus / Uranus (5/1-5)

I AM THAT WHICH...

helps to cultivate in you the ability to explore life without self-judgment so that all your life experiences might be seed-gifts for learning, resiliency and growth.

It is through your strivings and stumblings, seekings and findings that you can come to know and express more of the fullness of who you are. What interferes with and impedes that process is self-judgment. You are here to experience what you are drawn to, what you want, what you love—not what you or anyone else may think you should want or should be. Indeed, it is the shoulds of life which lead to self-judgment, which then makes the ever-truing self you seek recede and shrivel.

Are you hard on yourself when you don't perform to your own or others' expectations? Are the judges in your head the voices of others who have been disappointed in their own lives? Or the voices of static belief systems that have become disconnected from heart and the river of love that allows all life-affirming currents to be expressed in the circle of life in their true and right time? Do you think that by judging yourself you are pre-empting the judgment of others past, present or future—or of some distant fearsome God? How would you feel to know that there is no heavenly judge or condemnation in the realm of the Divine—only those you appoint and self-appoint in your time on Earth?

All seeming obstacles, stumbling stones or setbacks are opportunities to play with different hues in the very wondrous and colorful palette of hue-man experience. Embrace every new sojourn within your life-journey for the gifts of experience, insight and learning along your way. Don't let judgment of self or others deprive you of the wonders of living. Spend less time in condemnation of others, and more time and heart in actions of love that can help to change the things in your world that foster the hurt, hate and anger that brings about so much loss and sorrow.

Forgiveness is needed on Earth because you judge yourselves and each other so mercilessly when trust in love is overcome by fear. And thus, draw upon my light as HAZIEL to be lovingly merciful and compassionate with yourself, so that you might lighten your life on Earth and the lives of all you meet. For both within and beyond the context of your physical consciousness, there is only the desire of your soul to keep growing and evolving. There are no mistakes; there is only learning. There is no failure, only the chance to try again in a different way. There is no loser, losing or being lost—only the sometimes long and winding road to get there. And as you walk, run, crawl, leap or fly through every step and day of your life, let your light not be dimmed—for your light is our light, and ours is yours.

So dear beloved, have mercy on yourself and each other, for in mercy's light, there is ultimately nothing to forgive! Amen...

10 ALADIAH

(ah-LAH-dee-YAH)
Divine Grace (G)
'One who endows you with the yes of life'
Archangel ~ RAZIEL
Taurus / Saturn (5/6-10)

I AM THAT WHICH...

helps you to open your heart to the gift of Presence that can give you a sense of wonder and possibility for more in your life than current circumstances might reveal.

*Grace is not a thing earned or won by merit or manipulation. Grace is a sacred visitation unto your willing heart. To receive the grace that is gifted to you by the Divine is to know that you are known and inhabited by the Divine Itself—even when you don't **feel** Its Presence. Nevertheless, the Divine is always **here in this moment** with and within you, as you can know and feel when you become utterly present.*

Through grace, you are given the love and compassion to address the needs, desires and expressions of your different parts and purposes. To honor the gift of grace that comes to you, treat yourself with that same love. Listen to your heart-truth and let it guide both your small and great life choices. Heed the desire of your soul for meaning and purpose in your life expressions. Nourish your body and listen to its signals for what it needs health and well-being. Keep your mind open and malleable to the greater knowing of your heart and soul. Allow your inner to be expressed in your outer, and bring your outer into your inner for greater understanding of the life around you and your place and purpose in it.

Living with grace is to not push and pull at life, but to feel and attune with the cyclical flow of coming and going that is natural to

73

the seasons of life. Revel in life's beauties and bold expressions, and also be attentive to the subtleties that bring gifts of understanding. Allow your moods to be as passing ships and do not harbor resentment, guilt or shame, but rather see the opportunities for new creations in disappointment, and undertake to correct infractions as soon as you can so that you do not continue to carry their weight. Be patient and forgiving of yourself, and it will be easier to do so with others.

Through grace, you become not just a survivor of your hurts, but born anew through healing and transformation. With grace, you ride gently upon the winds of time as you come to know that you are more than the circumstances of your past, present or future. In the rarer ethers of grace, you may feel the breath of the Divine continually breathing into being more and more of your sacred and true Divine-Human self.

I, ALADIAH, am the gentle grace-light that illuminates and renews the gifts of Spirit within you daily and moment to moment. Allow my light to lighten your life, to replace the places of heaviness with the things of heaven, the darkness with light, and to help you ease the weight of life's demands and responsibilities. Thus you may embrace the colors of your own divinely 'hue-man' being which compose the rainbow of your ongoing becoming. So may it be. Amen...

11 LAUVIAH

(LOH-vee-YAH)
Victory (G)
'One who turns every moment into a win'
Archangel ~ RAZIEL
Taurus / Jupiter (5/11-15)

I AM THAT WHICH...

helps you to 'win' at being you by allowing your Divine and Human parts to work together to bring more and more of who you truly and uniquely are into manifestation.

You are infinitely creative and capable by virtue of the eternal which resides within you. However, the context of your physical life is time and place, and so you must make choices every day about what, when, where, why and how much. It is easy to regret the road you didn't take or the thing you didn't do—unless you understand who you are, what matters most to you and what you really want. As frustrating as the seeming limitations of life may be, you chose to come to Earth <u>because</u> of them—because they help to provide focus and direction, and because the contrasts and challenges of life help to stimulate creativity and cooperation between your inner and outer resources.

You are here to create a victorious life—a life in which the Divine-Human aspects of your personal 'I Am' work in tandem to achieve the purposes, goals and desires of your whole being. This means that all your parts—soul-heart-mind-body—must be considered in your choices; otherwise, they will become alienated from each other as they struggle for expression, or even dominance—while your self-conflict is played out externally. An example of this might be a conflict you feel about career options— perhaps your heart and soul call you to writing or art, but the

75

practical voices within or around you urge you toward a business career where you might make more money. If you can think of your possibilities as "and" rather than "either/or," you will likely find ways in which you can do both, if both are truly important to you. For ultimately, while the Earth-plane is a playground for creativity, exploration and discovery, the only truly authentic 'win' in life is to win at being you by bringing more and more of who you are into being and expression. And this is a win so utterly personal to you that no one but you can determine or achieve it.

There is so much in your societies which plays to the notion of being either a winner or a loser. But this two-dimensional way of perceiving the value of yourselves and each other shortchanges all at every level. The true and important victories in life ultimately come not through things you are able to acquire or even achieve, but what you are willing to give and receive, what you stand for as a testament to who you are and what you love. Those are the lasting and reverberating victories that generate new life within and around you. And so, listen...feel...dare to fully be. Not in a fixed or stubborn way, but in ways that take the most courage—to give what you love both voice and choice in your life, and thereby allow your truths to grow and even change. It is this kind of courage that will return you to yourself every time the world pulls you away, because it does and it will.

Dear one, I tell you as LAUVIAH that you are here as a walker of two worlds—the worlds of the unseen and the seeable: the inner-outer, eternity-time, Heaven and Earth realms of your soul-body being which must cooperate together in order for you to come into your fullness. Thus, your Earthly task is not to choose between them, but to utilize the resources of both by letting your Divine-Human parts be partners in this great 'pas-de-deux' of your life. For your ultimate 'win-win' is that both your divinity and your humanity might be fulfilled with, and because of, each other—and in so doing enable you to become one with yourself, and with Life Itself. So may it be. Amen...

12 HAHAIAH

(hah-HAH-ee-YAH)
Refuge, Shelter (G)
'One who is a beacon of shelter within'
Archangel ~ RAZIEL
Taurus / Mars (5/16-20)

I AM THAT WHICH...

brings awareness of the eternal refuge within every present moment, and within the heart of yourself and what matters most, so that you may have shelter and comfort wherever you are in the external world.

Places and times of refuge are important in Earth-life, because your life here is so very demanding on your energy and attention. However, there may be times when you feel pulled in different directions, between seemingly opposing desires or demands, and being not quite 'here nor there.' You may feel sometimes that you are 'going nowhere,' or even that you belong nowhere in your world. But the refuge in nowhere is always 'now-here'—the here and now of the present moment, which can give you shelter and comfort no matter where you are or what pulls at you. Right here and now you can find yourself, and be found.

The present is an ongoing opportunity to relinquish the past and allow the future to unfold in its own due time. Without preoccupation with the past or the future, you become fully available for the gifts, the presents/presence of not only what is right in front of you, but inside you. And here, in your own within, is a whole world of possibility which includes the powers and greater knowings of the eternal realms that you may access for a greater quality of life in the temporal realm of Earth. For ultimately, the present is the doorway to your true home, the home of your Divine-Human heart, which carries within it the personal truth of your soul and its purposes and potentials for this lifetime.

Sometimes the true and right decisions cannot be made by thinking them through; rather they must be felt by heart and 'gut'—with the intuition and instinctual knowing that comes from feeling, wisdom, and body intelligence—and a sense of yourself as connected to a greater whole that is both universal and deeply personal. Not that your mind shouldn't weigh in, but ideally in tandem with the vital information that comes from your heart-truth and body-knowing—what you really feel and want without any of the 'shoulds' or 'what-ifs' with which the mind is often so preoccupied.

It will help you to know what you want if you remember what you love. The refuge of meditation, prayer, communion with the natural world, sleep and dreams can help you to move past your conscious or unconscious worries, concerns, fears or conditionings, and reveal the truth of yourself, your feelings, and what matters to you. Even if you do not remember or understand your dreams, especially when they engage the timeless layers of your soul-being, they, like sleep itself, do their healing work within you nevertheless. So do a sense of home and connection with loved ones, physical exercise, spiritual practice, creativity, and any enjoyment that helps you return to yourself.

Dear one, I invite you to use my light as HAHAIAH to help you find safe haven and 'time-out' in any moment of your life when it is needed. In this, as you make your Angelically-lighted way from any seeming nowhere to now-here, which can take you anywhere, may you find refuge and shelter everywhere. Amen...

13 YEZALEL

(YAY-zah-LEL)
Fidelity, Loyalty and Allegiance (G)
'One who keeps faith with the inner Divine'
Archangel ~ RAZIEL
Gemini / Sun (5/21-25)

I AM THAT WHICH...

helps you to be faithful to the feeling, truth and wisdom of your heart as the confidant of your soul, and to discern and heed its voice over all the other voices within and around you.

There may be many voices in your life, both inner and outer, that clamor for your attention and allegiance. Some voices are loud and unmistakable, and some you may have lived with for so long that you don't realize how you are continually affected and influenced— even fragmented and diminished—by their constant insinuation. Know this, however: you empower all the voices in your life, whether inspirational or diminishing, by your choice to listen and your beliefs about yourself.

Your true-heart voice is always the one that not only accepts, but loves who you are, even while you are becoming more of who you want to be. It does not nitpick or pull at pieces of you, but puts you back together with compassion again and again toward wholeness and well-being. This innermost voice illuminates your beauty both seen and unseen, and supports the uniqueness of who you are ever striving to be with the gifts you have been given to do so.

Your true-heart voice will never shame or doubt you or make you feel smaller or afraid. It will never ask you to banish or suppress some part of yourself to obey something or someone else, or even to bring something 'higher' through you. It will never tell you that you are weak or 'only human' or contaminated by sin. Your true-heart

79

voice will show you that you are here on Earth with a mission: to incarnate the Light of Love and Truth in a glorious configuration of spirit-heart-mind-body with which you may bring learning and fulfillment to all parts of your Divine-Human beingness and for betterment to your world.

We suggest for you to consider every voice in your life that has impact on the feelings you hold about yourself, and to measure them by the Divine Light that sees and knows you truly and lovingly, no matter—and even because of—the where, what, when, how and why of your life and being. In all your worldly loyalties, let none pull you from loyalty to yourself and the greater knowing of love and truth that reside within you, as you. And if any should try to do so, simply return to the self you are in the very heart of you and let them be in the 'outer circles' of your life. Keep close company only with those who encourage and inspire you to be more and more yourself. Yet, forgive those who cannot see or appreciate you—because it may be that they cannot appreciate themselves, or that they simply don't have the 'bandwith' to see you at this moment in time.

And so dear beloved one, keep faith with my YEZALEL light that you may always return in faithfulness to your own inner truths. For it is the 'still small voice' within you that our Angelic Presences amplify to cultivate your listening and to get your attention when you're not! 'To thine own self be true,' for loyalty to yourself is an expression of your fidelity and allegiance to your own soul and the Divine from which it was born.

This is how you do justice to yourself, your life, and the gifts you carry within you, and which shall be created by you, to give unto your world. So may it be. Amen...

14 MEBAHEL

(MAY-bah-HEL)
Truth, Liberty and Justice (G)
'One who is freed by Love to set Truth free'
Archangel ~ RAZIEL
Gemini / Venus (5/26-31)

I AM THAT WHICH...

helps you to be free to express and live your own truths, and to allow love to keep evolving them into new expressions of life.

There is nowhere in your whole being or world that holds, and evolves, your truths more profoundly and relevantly than your own heart. Thus the ultimate justice—and justness—for your life is not about what others accord you, but if you are willing to be guided by what you truly value and want for your own life. This is the ultimate freedom, and the ultimate way to 'do justice' to your time on Earth. For if you let the values, needs and wants of others continually eclipse what you want for your own life, then you are not free. This can result in anxiety, fear, anger, depression, shame, guilt and doubt, which can further muffle your personal truths until they recede from your consciousness.

Your inner truths have many ways of letting you know when you aren't paying attention to them. To speak about depression 'non-clinically,' we suggest that prolonged suppression, or denial of expression, of one's personal truths underlies many depressive states of being. When a personal truth slips off the table of your options, even for 'important' or 'practical' reasons, you can suffer a perpetual feeling of being trapped 'between a rock and a hard place' with no seemingly viable possibility for joy or thriving. If you have decided that living your truth is not an option, then you may find yourself in the impossible situation of having to choose between things you don't really want. That's not what you chose this life for—and your depression may be your soul letting you know that it needs to be listened to.

'But what about needs and responsibilities?' you may interject. We say, as you do, that 'there are many ways to skin the cat!' When you are not in the right relationship, job or circumstance for your thriving, but either fear of change or a sense of 'responsibility' keeps you tethered, it's time to get creative. You can have what you truly want—but you may have to think and act 'outside the box' of habitual or 'normal' thinking or behavior. Perhaps scary at first, but your willingness will give loft to quantum leaps that may seem unimaginable or undoable before you take that first step.

Each time you express your truth, not only does 'the truth set you free,' but that truth is itself freed to become a new truth. You may experience this especially if you speak a truth that has been long-hidden—only to feel in the speaking a sudden release as if it weren't even true or relevant anymore. In doing justice to an old truth by expressing it, you free it to evolve into a truth that is more relevant and dynamic with your present beingness—which in turn frees you from a truth that belongs to the past. In being freed from what was, you can move toward the truth of your present and future potential.

Dear one, if you are a truth-lover, let my light as MEBAHEL help to free you from old stories about who you are, or a thought that you should be anyone other than yourself! You are not on this Earth 'to follow a star in someone else's sky.' To be and express your own ever-evolving true self is to do justice to your life, and by example help to make the world a more true and just place for all.

So shining one, take up the mantle of your light and sparkle unto the world, so that your courage of self may inspire others who also long to be 'brave-hearts' in their own true-self making. Shine forth, and be not dimmed by those who cannot bear your light in the moment. For your radiance will help to awaken, perhaps in ways not for you to know, the light-seeds of their own trueness, in their own due time. Amen...

82

4/4 * **6/18** * 9/1 * 11/13 * 1/23

15 HARIEL

(HAH-ree-EL)
Purification (G)
'One who uses the light to wash clean'
Archangel ~ RAZIEL
Gemini / Mercury (6/1-5)

I AM THAT WHICH...

helps you to experience the Divine as a purifying Presence within, which supports you in becoming your 'best self' by taking in foods, atmospheres and associations that are nourishing, cleansing and life-affirming for your particular body and being.

Your best self is always your true self, and thus your 'purity' or 'goodness' is not about perfection according to any religious morality or social ideology. To be pure of heart is to be open to the soul of yourself and the inner Divine that your soul conveys to your heart through love, intuition, inspiration and the cultivation of wisdom. To be pure of mind is to value clarity, truth, knowledge and the guiding resources of the heart which transform knowledge into wisdom and give the mind a higher reach. To be pure of body is to partake of what your particular physicality needs for optimum nourishment, exercise and rest. In this rich personal atmosphere, there is no room for the harboring of hidden agendas, inner or outer saboteurs, attitudes, motives or relatings that might be disenfranchising or diminishing to yourself or others.

In the vibrational density and persuasiveness of human life, it is often impossible to <u>sustain</u> a state of purity. However, because you are essentially born of the Divine, your purity is intrinsic and always reclaimable. The Angelic Divine is given unto you to help you recover again and again your own true light and to be cleansed of energies and circumstances that muffle, dim or diminish you. Such

83

diminishment can start on the outside or the inside, but your emotions and your body reflect disturbances and conflicts on all levels, and thus can show you almost immediately where healing and clearing are needed.

Saying yes to life does not mean partaking of everything and everyone that comes along or allowing them all to partake of you; rather it means associating yourself with people and things that affirm and support the love and truth of who you are. Of course, things can happen that seem to be other people or circumstances acting upon you. But in those times, you can at the very least choose your response, and by that choice either compound a difficulty or diffuse it. Using challenges as opportunities to illuminate, refine and claim your own truths and desires ensures that you will always be able to return to purity of self no matter what occurs in your life.

And finally dear one, know this: Purity is not meant to be a yoke. The striving for purity at any level succeeds only when it proceeds from a sense of purpose and self-love rather than forced discipline, guilt, self-judgment, shame or pride. As the purifying light of HARIEL within and around you, I wish for you to enter into the gift of purity as it is Divinely-intended for you—as a daily-renewable opportunity for an unencumbered heart, mind and body, and a beautifully bearable lightness of being. Amen...

4/5 * **6/19** * 9/2 * 11/14 * 1/24

16 HAKAMIAH

(hah-KAH-mee-YAH)
Loyalty (G)
'One who aligns with the inner Divine'
Archangel ~ RAZIEL
Gemini / Moon (6/6-10)

I AM THAT WHICH...

helps you to walk a life path that honors your ever-evolving truth and what matters most to you, and to measure all outer calls for loyalty against your inner sense of what is true, right and life-affirming for the whole of you.

Loyalty to self is supported by the love of the Divine for you, dwelling within you. Understood in this light, self-love is not about selfishness, but rather 'selfulness'—a wholeness and harmony of self that honors your inner Divinity, and is cultivated and protected by Divine Love. This loving self-loyalty enables you to know instinctively what situations, people and energies affirm the truth of you—and to move toward those who welcome you rather than fight for the acceptance of those who don't. The more at ease you feel with honoring yourself, the less you will need to set fixed boundaries to guard against infringement—or feel guilty when you naturally assert what you need and want. Know this: the outer world will never be your 'enemy' when you are a true friend to yourself.

Loyalty does not have any value on its own; it takes its value from that which it supports. Loyalty to something or someone that goes against your truth and undermines you is rather a self-betrayal. This holds true especially when your desire for belonging to a particular tribe or group asks things of you that go against your values or what you truly want for your own life. If your first loyalty is to your own inner heart-and-soul truth, all worldly calls for your loyalty can be easily discerned as to their relevance and life-affirming rightness for you.

Every expression in your world begets more of itself, and it is entirely your choice what you multiply purposefully—or even accidentally or 'by default' in not choosing. In keeping faith with your higher values and principles in intent, word and deed, you may prevail against inner and outer energies or circumstances that might undermine your endeavors, your aspirations, and even your very being.

Also, in loyalty to the truth of yourself, realize that just as you are always becoming more of who you are, so will your truth evolve. Thus, let your self-loyalty have room for changing circumstances and perspectives about yourself, each other and the world. It is not fickleness, but wisdom, that changes your heart or mind when you have more information and experience. Furthermore, as you bring your inner truths to the world, know that every dawning of self-truth inspires the evolving truths of others, sooner or later, in their own true time.

I, HAKAMIAH, am the Divine Light given to illuminate for you that self-loyalty at its highest honors both your inner Divinity and the unique form of humanity that you embody on this privilege of Earth. When you claim this for the whole of you, your inner Divine as the very essence of Love Itself will be your protector and care for you while you care for others in ways that address your unique being. Thus may you be free to be a light in the lives of all you encounter that they may see how to claim this radiant worth within their own beings.

Blessed are you in your shining, and blessed are we to witness and support you. Amen...

June 20—June 27

Angels 17—24

Sephira 3

BINAH ~ Understanding

Overlighting Archangel

TZAPHKIEL ~ 'Beholder of the Divine'
Understanding of self and God, contemplation,
meditation and compassion

---

17 LAVIAH

18 CALIEL

19 LEUVIAH

20 PAHALIAH

21 NELCHAEL

22 YEIAYEL

23 MELAHEL

24 HAHEUIAH

17 LAVIAH

(LAH-vee-YAH)
Revelation (R)
'One who parts the veil'
Archangel ~ TZAPHKIEL
Gemini / Uranus (6/11-15)

I AM THAT WHICH...

helps to reveal the true you to yourself through your feelings and responses, and especially through dreamtime symbols and messages when you are untethered from ego and daily concerns, and more receptive to your soul-self and spirit guidance.

All the great revelations in your life have to do with discovering more of who you are, what matters and means most to you and why you are here. The reason so many of you are at a loss to know your purpose in life is because your purpose is revealed through what you love, what you have great feeling and passion for—and that criteria is not often at the top of your vetting list when you are looking for a 'responsible,' 'respectable,' 'successful' or "power" position in your society. Thus, you may sometimes experience yourself feeling as a 'stranger in a strange land,' with a nagging and restless sense of unbelonging or a perennial 'looking in all the wrong places' for something missing. What is missing is usually <u>some truth of yourself that is not being recognized or engaged</u>.

On a soul-level, you know who and why you are. The key in the density and soul-forgetting of Earth-life is to connect with your soul to access that remembering. For this, you have been provided with two great inner 'bridges.' The first is your heart, the receiver and broadcaster of your soul and its limitless resources. Your heart has tremendous capacity for feeling the many hues of love, compassion, joy, caring, and also sadness. And it is also able to commingle love,

89

knowledge, experience and intuition in order to cultivate wisdom. As the 'confidante' and messenger for the indwelling Divine spark that is your soul, your heart is a guide for your life. It is your soul-infused heart that expresses a unique configuration of Divine attributes within your human beingness, brings meaning and purpose to your life, and is your lifeline to the eternal realm of Spirit. As your 'soul-stuff' is continually broadcast to your heart, you always have the Divine 'on tap' at this, your innermost altar where your humanity may drink of your inner Divinity. Thus, 'there where your heart is, shall your treasure be.'

A second inner bridge that reveals more of yourself, your potentials and purposes, is your dreamtime. During sleep, when your physical mind and body are loosened from the preoccupations of ego and daily concerns, you are more receptive to your eternal soul-self and to those in the 'other-worlds' who can give you guidance if you desire. Much information forgotten in your waking life is held in your 'soulular' memory, as well as in the 'memory banks' of your under-consciousness—both of which you can more easily access when your body and everyday mind are in a relaxed state. During dreamtime, and also meditation, you can work with the whole spectrum of your soul and its many manifestations of personality. As a soul-body being, you are a walker of two worlds. Thus, the awarenesses that emerge in your dreamtime, meditative or dream-like states can help to create a bridge between the worlds— the one you came from and the one you are visiting—so that you may ultimately feel greater ease with being and expressing more of your totality during your time on Earth.

Dear one, use my light as LAVIAH to guide you across these waking and sleeping bridges and to incorporate into your conscious being and doing the revelations offered to you from within. Look at yourself through our eternal Angel-eyes to see why you are an important expressive and ever-evolving piece in the bigger picture of All That Is, Has Been and Will Be in both time and eternity. Amen...

18 CALIEL

(KAH-lee-EL)
Justice (S)
'One who sustains cosmic laws for all'
Archangel ~ TZAPHKIEL
Gemini / Saturn (6/16-21)

I AM THAT WHICH...

helps you to act justly on behalf of yourself and to heal issues that may cause you to be overly vulnerable to disrespect or unjustness from others.

All justice that you may look for in the world must start within yourself, toward yourself and for yourself. You are here to live your life not only for the fulfillment of your humanity, but also for the expression of your inner Divinity. You are born justified because you carry within you a constellation of qualities that are aspects of the Divine Itself, and because of your courage to submit your Divinity to this human challenge—and adventure—of time and place.

When you are co-creating life with your inner Divine, you will not always feel the need to look to the world for justness and justice. But for those moments when you feel sorrow or anger for having been treated unjustly by any person or circumstance, look first to any unjustness with which you treat yourself. No matter how it may look to others, an accuser cannot harm you unless you are already accusing yourself. You cannot be humiliated unless you already feel ashamed, nor dominated unless you have relinquished your self-sovereignty. No person or circumstance has any power over you unless you have already abdicated your own. We do not speak of self-fault here, but the natural laws of 'like attracts like.'

People often treat others as badly as they treat themselves—or sometimes much better! But when you treat yourself and others

91

justly and with dignity and respect, you show them 'how it is done.'
They may not get it the first time, or the tenth, but you will have
planted a seed that will blossom in their own time of realization.
When it is you who have treated others unjustly, guard against the
misuse of conscience. Do not indulge the inner accusers, judges,
shame and guilt which can paralyze true responsibility and
corrective action. Be grateful that life has given you an opportunity
to practice the art of apology—and set things right!

It is so much easier to be human when you allow the Divine
within you to live life with you and through you! In your Divine-
Human isness, you are justified and valued just as you are,
vulnerability and all, as a unique expression of the Love-and-Truth
Light that is the Divine Itself. Thus, no matter what you may suffer
in this life, whatever seeming injustice is laid upon you or against
you, you will know that you are worthy and valuable to life beyond
measure. Your very existence brings something to the world that
cannot be found in all the universes except through you. Therefore,
honor yourself and what you need for your sovereignty. Let not your
mind be frayed, your emotions manipulated, nor your dignity
splintered by judgment of yourself or the judgments and attitudes of
others. Look for justice first in the love and truth of your own heart
and soul, and it will come to you from the world, sooner or later, in
ways perhaps least expected but entirely suited to what you signed
up for!

I, CALIEL, and we Angelically all, hold the primordial Light of
Divine Love and Truth in the well of your heart. Herein you may
draw from it when you have forgotten what a treasure you are to
the Greatness that birthed you, which has never left you. Even now
It is sustaining and communing with you through these words and
the infinite Love that words cannot fully convey. Amen...

19 LEUVIAH

(LOO-vee-YAH)
Expansive Intelligence & Fruition (G)
'One who uses heart to quicken soul memory and higher mind'
Archangel ~ TZAPHKIEL
Cancer / Jupiter (6/22-26)

I AM THAT WHICH...

helps you to see your own potential in the reflections and messages of the natural world and to use every encounter as a way to broaden your intelligence, understanding and inner-outer fulfillment.

Imagine your mind branching out and up into the light of possibility like the wide-canopied treetops reach toward a bright summer sky. Imagine that everything is more than you might even imagine it to be—and that all of life is ever inviting YOU to make something more of it by making more of yourself.

Everything in the natural world is not only itself, but a reflection and beckoning of your own potential. As the artists and poets among you have long been inspired by, the flora and fauna of nature are as 'codes' of metaphor and meaning expressed through their forms and functions. Like the tree with its deep roots and reaching branches that symbolize your own need to be grounded while you branch out into life and reach up for the rarer light of your dreams and desires. Or the flowers in summer that blossom with every color under the sun, as the 'hue-man' you are delights in the cultivation of your own true colors and those of your loved ones—and, ideally, the diversity of all species and beings on Earth. Or the winged sky creatures that give your imaginings loft and urge you toward your own flights of fancy and the near or far horizons of your unique dreams. Or the bees that buzz around you, challenging you to either get busy or to

93

leave off your busy or anxious ways for a moment to just 'bee' in presence!

Everything, literally everything, holds a message, a gift—a present—for you when you bring yourself into the ever-present fullness of life with your own presence!

When you are here in the now, you are able to access the powers of the eternal to help you listen and attune to not only what is said or presented, but what has yet been unspoken or unmanifested. To receive the presence of another with an atmosphere of openness and possibility, without imposing your own conditionings and belief systems, is an energetic invitation that will ultimately reveal the 'more than meets the eye' of the other—and you. For you and each and all of life are so much more than you ever seem to be—and thus the possibilities of your life and relatings will never cease to be rich and wondrous if you allow space among you for mutual emergence. Expand your inner world—your awareness, your willingness, your presence of heart and mind, and you will contribute to the expansion of your outer world as greater possibilities for yourself and all.

And so I, LEUVIAH, invite you to descend deep into the well of your heart and drink of my light-cup that is ever brimming with the shimmer of your expanding possibility. With every 'sip' from the font of my Divine Light, allow more of yourself to be illuminated, lightened and enlightened. Allow the flow of giving and receiving to move through your heart unceasingly. Allow love and life to bring you more and more into fruition for your own Divine-Human fulfillment, and as an inspiration for others to do the same, in their own different ways and due times.

Thus will your soul take root in your heart, in your mind and in your body in ways most beautiful! Amen...

20 PAHALIAH

(pah-HAH-lee-YAH)
Redemption (G)
'One who restores the Self'
Archangel ~ TZAPHKIEL
Cancer / Mars (6/27-7/1)

I AM THAT WHICH...

helps you to practice the true and loving principles of redemption by reclaiming your heart and soul from choices and actions that are not of your true nature so that your life might have the depth and meaning that your humanity longs for.

Every human being has the desire for a meaningful life, whether aware of it or not. For this, your life must reflect not only quantity of experience, but quality—and quality is in the arena of the heart and soul, which hold your true values and purposes and give your life a sense of meaning and worthwhileness. In your beautiful yet often noisy and compelling world, it can be hard to hear the whispered truths of your inner voices. Yet, living without their input has its consequences. Sometimes the effects accumulate, slowly separating your parts from each other, dampening joy and enthusiasm for your life and causing existential anxiety about identity, meaning and purpose. And if this continues for too long, depression and physical illness can occur.

Your heart is the confidant of your soul and the amplifier of its voice to all your other parts. As the bridge between your inner Divinity and your humanity, your heart broadcasts not only the purposes of your soul, but also its frustration and discomfort at not being heard or heeded. And so, we say, listen to your heart and you will hear your soul. The intuitions and truths of your heart are a commingling of information from your soul and your humanity—

and your feelings are the barometer of whether you are heeding these or not. Thus, be aware of and responsive to your feelings. Follow the feeling, and it will show you the cause. Find the cause and you will see where healing is needed. While the softness of your flesh is both your outer vulnerability and protector of your inner physiology, the softness of your heart is both your inner vulnerability and the strength of your whole being.

True redemption is not about 'saving you from your sins,' but saving your heart and soul from the effects upon them of the more vibrationally dense physical world. The paradox of life is that you must continually reclaim yourself—your Self—from the world, even while using the world as a creative space to manifest your soul purposes. How do you do that? Not by controlling the world around you, but by modulating your reactions to the world, exercising your right to choose, being present to your own needs and desires, and doing things that give you a sense of well-being. Smile at people, be kind, let the person behind you go in front, help someone, commune with nature, listen to your favorite music. See the opportunity in a setback, the gift in a disappointment and the potential gain in a seeming loss. You are part of life and life is part of you, and these connective actions can 'redeem' your deeper, truer self from the challenges and stresses of daily living.

Thus dear one, I offer you my PAHALIAH light to help you reclaim, as in take yourself back, from anything that takes you away from who you are at heart—and want to become more of. Many 'sins of the world' are brought about by those who are acting as who they are not, because they are disconnected from heart and thus cut off from the Divinity of soul. And so your redemption, again and again, is to return inward to that truest, softest place within, and dare to listen. Dare to kneel down in self-compassion and humility. And dare to be led by the love and truth of your own being which is cradled here in this, the innermost altar of your heart. Amen...

21 NELCHAEL

(NEL-kah-EL)
Ardent Desire to Learn (G)
'One who inspires delight in learning'
Archangel ~ TZAPHKIEL
Cancer / Sun (7/2-6)

I AM THAT WHICH...

amplifies in you a passion for learning about yourself and the areas that are most relevant to your heart's desires and soul purposes, which reflect those aspects of the Divine that you have come to Earth to embody and express.

There is so much in the world to fascinate your mind's curiosity, and there are endless opportunities for learning many different kinds of things. And you will find along the way that your true interests can be awakened, or renewed, by even the smallest, seeming irrelevant bits of information. Yet, while early in life you may be urged to explore everything that comes your way, ultimately you have come to Earth to focus your intelligence and creativity in areas that express your soul purposes and make more of the particular and unique Divine-Human being that you are. And thus, we invite you to use our 'enthusiasm of light' to help you bring more soul-awareness into your heart, mind and body in order to discern what is most relevant to the ways of love, truth and purpose within you.

Your soul purposes seek affinity with your receptive heart—and your heart then seeks out affinity and feeling with people, things and circumstances in the world which are affirming and complementary to those purposes. Thus, the clues to your purposes will become more apparent by what you are drawn to, as well as your degree of enthusiasm, motivation and willingness to undertake the paths of invitation. Circumstances, people and ideas that appear in your path are always opportunities for you to learn more about yourself—both what you want and don't want, and who you more truly are versus the person you or others may expect or think you to be. For by virtue of the Divine that dwells within you, you are infinitely more capable than you might have ever imagined.

Patience and respect for your own learning and becoming is foundational to learning about your inner Divine nature. As a particular 'image and likeness' of the Divine, the totality of your being represents a unique constellation of Divine qualities that are vibrationally diverse enough to encompass both essence and form. (Thus the humus, or base mettle of your human substance and consciousness, might be understood as the heavier vibrations of 'Divine Light-Stuff.') And like stars and stones, or starlight and stardust, a fullness of life on Earth requires you to partake of both. As you grow and learn, more inner space opens up for the lighter aspects of the Divine to expand and be expressed within you—which then enables you to learn and become even more on the physical plane! This is the complementary co-creation of Divine-Human life.

Thus Who I AM as NELCHAEL says to you: Better on Earth to be a student than a master—so that there might be no limit to what you are willing and able to learn! With all our love, we urge you to show yourself the utmost kindness and humility while coming to know yourself by allowing space for the potentials of you that are still unfolding. Let yourself learn and grow without self-doubt or judgment—or the insecurity of arrogance that sometimes tries to mask not knowing. For the more you learn about your own nature, each other and the natural world, the more you will fathom about the seemingly fathomless Divine—and your unique role in bringing a bit of heaven to Earth through your own beautiful Divine-Human expression.

So it has always been, and so may it ever be, in time and throughout eternity. Amen...

22 YEIAYEL

(YAY-ah-YEL)
Fame, Renown (G)
'One who inspires knowing of Self'
Archangel ~ TZAPHKIEL
Cancer / Venus (7/7-11)

I AM THAT WHICH...

helps you to know who you are and be known to others by your authenticity and willingness to be true to your ever-evolving self, even in those times when you may not be accepted or understood.

Coming to know yourself involves inner and outer reflection and a combination of exploring, observing and expressing your own heart and mind in relation to others. As much as you might feel that you know yourself, it is often through relationship that even more of you is revealed and brought into being. Furthermore, to feel truly known by others helps to affirm not only that you exist, but that your existence is valuable. And so, the desire to be and feel known is compelling. Indeed, there are many who seek and experience renown in the greater world as well—but being famous does not mean that you know yourself, or are known for who you truly are, as many of your celebrities and public figures would attest.

Though you may actually be 'well-known'—or just a 'legend in your own mind,' as your humor would say—most of you want to be seen, heard, felt and known by at least your loved ones and friends. Not to be known is to live in loneliness—even if you are engaged in life in very outward and social ways. While you are utterly known by the Divine Itself, to be truly known in your world you must be willing to know yourself and allow others to know you. Self-knowing, or lack thereof, colors everything you do, everything you create that ripples out into the lives of others, and everything you leave in your wake. 'Know thyself,' the wise have said through the ages. But what does that mean, really, you might ask?

*To truly know yourself is to know that you are of Divine origin, made of uniquely configured Divine 'Stuff' in varying presentations of lighter and denser energies which compose your particular soul, heart, mind and body—each of which have important roles to play in manifesting the totality of YOU. Your **soul** is drawn from and conveys Spirit unto your heart as the love, truth and purpose of you; your **heart**, which is the 'confidante' of your soul and your inner wisdom-maker, 'feels' life and forms affinities of love, family and friendship, and also serves as your internal compass for personal truth, meaning, direction and connection, and transmits those to the rest of your being; your **mind**—which is so much greater when working in tandem with your heart and soul—gathers, sorts, stores, retrieves and computes information and memories to generate thoughts, perceptions, ideas and sensibilities about life; and your **body** gives all your other parts 'a leg to stand on' and a way for your soul to be and do on this privilege of Earth. With self-knowledge of your 'on-board' resources, you may co-create a Divine-Human experience of life on Earth in ways that are unique to you and like no other.*

And so I, YEIAYEL, and all your Angelic light-mates, tell you that in coming to know the Divine-Human ways and wonders of yourself, you can realize that there is always so much more to know about you than can be known through appearances—and that more will unfold and evolve throughout your time here. The same is true about others—and if you truly want to know the uniqueness of each other, you must dive beneath the surface to see not only the humanity of each of you, but also your inner Divinity.

Thus are our Angelic luminations given to you so that you might know more and more of yourself and to recognize the multi-faceted light of the One shining from within your unique attributes and the beautiful and sacred diversities of all. Amen...

4/12 * **6/26** * 9/9 * 11/21 * 1/30

23 MELAHEL

(MAY-lah-HEL)
Healing Capacity (G)
'One who shows where healing is possible'
Archangel ~ TZAPHKIEL
Cancer / Mercury (7/12-16)

I AM THAT WHICH...

helps you to partake of the natural world's substances, energies and elements for healing and renewing your body and being throughout the cycles of your life.

All elemental aspects within the natural world have either physical or essential vibrational presence in your own human nature in order to sustain your physiological life and convey resources and wisdoms for your resiliency and thriving. These include: **water**, *which quenches your physical thirst and provides flow for your bodily humors, emotions and inner/outer cleansing;* **earth**, *for the nutrition and humus of your body, providing grounding and rootedness to your whole being as well as herbs and medicinal plants for the formulation of natural remedies;* **air** *for your breath of life, clear and discerning thoughts and the winds of change that clear out the old to make way for the new; and* **fire**, *as bodily warmth, light and the awakening of passion and new life, as well as the sparks of initiative that inspire you to begin again and again through creativity and innovation.*

The natural world provides resources and nurturing for human life and well-being, as well as teachings for human nature and the wisdom of living. Thus, we invite you to learn from your beautiful Earth and partake of her powers of healing and regeneration. Heed the messages that each species of flora and fauna offer about interdependence, resiliency and ongoingness through the seasons

101

and cycles of birthing, growing, maturing, transforming and rebirthing.

Your body and psyche are continually working to heal even the small stresses, demands and distractions of your daily life. Your capacity to heal is directly related to your willingness to heal—to allow and co-create your own healing with the inner and outer resources you have been given to do just that. Just as in cooperating, even collaborating, with the natural world, if you embrace and nurture the riches of your own diverse nature, you and your creations will flourish and bring life-affirming energies to yourself, others and the world at large.

We suggest to put on your daily 'to-do' list some time for being. Bring your attention into the present with self-compassion and heartfulness, and allow whatever time and timelessness you need for rest and renewal. Thus, whatever difficulties or challenges may come, you will be better able to address them from an inner atmosphere of equilibrium and well-being.

Thus do I, MELAHEL, invite you to use my light to become aware of the things you can do daily and moment-to-moment to strengthen your healing capacity, starting with breathing and bringing yourself back to the present each time you think about a past or future moment with regret or worry. Take your 'what-ifs' for a walk in nature. Breathe the life force of the forest into any stressful and stifling thoughts, and let them go as you exhale. Be present with the presences of nature in humility and gratitude, and they will receive and transmute what needs healing, and transmit back to you resiliency and rejuvenation.

Know this, dear one, that there is dignity—we say again—dignity, in self-care and compassion, and embracing these for yourself will give those around you 'permission' to do the same, each in their own ways. Amen...

4/13 * **6/27** * 9/10 * 11/22 * 1/31

24 HAHEUIAH

(hah-HOO-ee-YAH)
Protection (G)
'One who is the keeper of true-selfness'
Archangel ~ TZAPHKIEL
Cancer / Moon (7/17-22)

I AM THAT WHICH...

helps to magnify the energies of love and truth within you as natural attractors of what is beneficial to your well-being—and a repellent to that which is not.

The more you are true and respectful to yourself and trust yourself to be so, the less you will feel the need to contrive protective barriers and boundaries between you and others. For it is important to realize that when you put up protective shields, they may not only keep out what you don't want, but also what you do want.

For example, putting a wall around your heart to keep anyone from hurting you can also keep out someone who wants to love you. To protect yourself from harm with tokens or talismans is also to distance yourself from reliance on the Divine that guards you from within—and from learning through all things that come your way. To protect yourself from pain or the unexpected 'what-ifs' of life can also make you less available for the joyful magic of serendipity and surprise. To protect yourself or your land from your neighbor's encroachment can discourage brotherhood and companionship. To protect yourself from the differences of others is to deprive you of the inspiration and complement of diversity and the discovery of your samenesses of heart. To refrain from fully living in an effort to protect yourself from the world's ills may also harbor the fear that invites them.

103

It is good to be alert to what is around you, but know, as many who live in volatile areas do, that to live in a constant state of self-protectiveness—for any reason, even a reasonable one—takes a toll on your happiness, your health and a wholesome sense of exploration and discovery that gives life its sparkle. Better not to show the universe that you expect to be hurt, which can energetically invite that very thing to happen. And once you begin to 'collect' and harbor injustices or 'bad-luck' events, no matter how many protections you put up they will keep coming at you to add to your collection and support your ongoing story!

We don't mean to say 'throw caution to the wind.' Rather, be wise but not worried. Be trusting, but not naïve. For if you trust yourself, your own motivations—and especially your resiliency—you will not need to worry about how and when others, or life itself, may seem to fall short of your expectations. Saying yes to life is to allow life to 'bring it on'—while you rely on the regenerating powers of the Love you are made of to use whatever comes your way for the growth and greaterness of your being.

And so dear one, I invite you to call upon my HAHEUIAH light to amplify your own soul-light so that the love and truth of you may shine forth as your greatest protection against anything or anyone, inner or outer, that would dim your light. For always you are best protected not by barricading your door against the dark, but by increasing your light.

And as your joy of being and doing radiates out from your within, those beings or things which do not belong with you will turn or fade away—and you will surely quicken the light of those who remain! So may it be. Amen...

June 28—July 6

Angels 25—32

Sephira 4

CHESED ~ Love/Mercy

Overlighting Archangel

TZADKIEL ~ 'Justice of God'
Mercy and kindness, beneficence,
grace, transmutation

---

25 **NITH-HAIAH**

26 **HAAIAH**

27 **YERATEL**

28 **SEHEIAH**

29 **REIYEL**

30 **OMAEL**

31 **LECABEL**

32 **VASARIAH**

25 NITH-HAIAH

(NIT-hah-YAH)
Spiritual Wisdom and Magic (R)
'One who quickens the abracadabra of life'
Archangel ~ TZADKIEL
Leo / Uranus (7/23-27)

I AM THAT WHICH...

helps more of your authentic self to appear on the stage of your life and to shine as the star you are in the Divine-Human 'light show' that is played out through the expression of your desires, dreams, potentials and purposes.

All the magic you need for a fulfilling life is conjured in being and expressing more of who you are by tapping the Divinity within your humanity. There is always more of you on your way from the eternal into time. As your Angelic light-assistants, we would direct you to stand stage center in your story, play an authentic role in every scenario, and surround yourself with cast-mates in co-lead and supporting roles who help your presence (and the presence of each) to be magnified rather than diminished. Use both protagonists <u>and</u> antagonists to define and strengthen your character—and follow the cues for new story lines that changing life scenarios provide you! To play your ever-truing self, without mask or script (especially someone else's), quickens a magical flow in not only your own life story, but also in the life stories of everyone around you. For trueness in one inspires trueness in others.

Each of you are here to follow a star in the sky of your own heart, to walk the path to which your inner light calls you, and to offer the treasures of your uniqueness to the world. For this is how the Divine comes to Earth—through you, and as the <u>particularity</u> of you! This is the gift of you that keeps on giving: the more you shine, the greater your capacity to be a light for others. For the <u>ultimate urge of true</u>

individuation for every 'hue-man' being is to be of service through the unique 'hues' of your nature—and to experience how the contribution of your own true colors makes the world more beautiful and meaningful. In fleshing out the purposes of your soul on Earth, you come to understand that here you are a unique commingling of Divine Light and the darker humus of matter, which is just a denser vibration that enables light to have form. In the embrace of your Divine-Human beingness, your presence can awaken the Divinity within others, which is a magical thing indeed!

The keepers of spiritual magic are the inner-seeing ones—the magi and Merlins, spiritual alchemists and 'high priests' of art and science, and the thinkers, feelers, seers and inspirers among you who see and do not turn away from the 'more than meets the eye' of beings and things. To count yourself among them is simply to see with the eyes of your heart, for the magic of the heart is that it sees all, both in and out of time. Thus, only with heart-seeing may you know the mysteries and magic of yourself or another, meet beings and events with compassion, and transform the impossible to the possible. For the heart can penetrate the veils of time, limitation, fact and circumstance with love enough to bring the powers of the eternal into time—and to follow all 'known facts' to their underlying causes and dare to change them. The heart can sense the dynamic energies among people, things and the Earth itself—how each increases or decreases the other, how and why each plays a part none other can play, and how to come together with others to create something greater than the sum of all.

So dear one holding the mysteries of the universe within the love and truth of you, may you partake of my NITH-HAIAH mage-light in your heart to go forth and be magical and wise from within. Bring your true and loving self unto your day in all you meet, say and do. Allow yourself to shine as a beacon of light on the vast stage of life so that you, and the Divine Itself, may know the magic and miracle of what it means to be you! Amen...

26 HAAIAH

(HAH-ee-YAH)
Political Science and Ambition (R)
'One who inspires cooperative expression'
Archangel ~ TZADKIEL
Leo / Saturn (7/28-8/1)

I AM THAT WHICH...

helps to support your soul's ambition to pursue higher truths and purposes by modulating excessive impulses of desire and thought, and cultivating an internal order that promotes cooperation and well-being among your bodily systems and subtle energies.

The term 'body politic' is usually applied to an organization or nation. However, so is each individual a 'body politic'—an amalgam of diverse aspects and hierarchies of essence, forms and functions that are all vital to the healthy whole of you. Every human being is composed of an inner (soul-self) and outer (personality-self), which are bridged by the dynamics of the heart-mind 'matrix.' It is the desire of your soul to cooperate with the denser humus of your physicality to create a magnificence of life that neither soul nor 'soil' could experience without the other. In the soul's corner is your heart, and in personality's corner is your mind. We suggest that the 'political order' that is most beneficial to your total well-being and fulfillment, as well as your contribution to society, is one in which your heart and soul compose the visionary 'executive branch,' and your mind/body/personality as the production and 'worker' branch. In addition, your body is also the barometer for how well all the parts are cooperating, or not. When all your parts are working in harmony, you will experience any outer stressors and conflicts more as interesting challenges rather than setbacks or defeats. Although soul and personality may sometimes seem to have opposing agendas, a more noble 'politics of life' will advance your soul's ambition to

109

express itself in all your being and doing—which then naturally enhances the capabilities, functioning and fulfillment of your humanity.

What is important to realize is that the clarity of your vision is vital to your ability to carry it out. If your vision is muddied by conflicting thoughts, emotions, urges or influences, then the part of you that tries to act is nullified or weakened—as if 'the rug is pulled out from under you' or you've been 'cut off at the knees.' This also plays out in groups and organizations when there isn't a clear organizing principle at the helm, or the executive branch is beleaguered by conflicting interests and dissent rather than collaborating on a unified vision with clear goals.

All that said, it is common for your 'soul-stuff' to become muffled because in the denser vibrations of physical beingness, soul consciousness is dimmed. Your attention easily becomes consumed with not only basic survival, but also with attraction to matter, the perks and pitfalls of free will and the development of ego which can both facilitate and compromise individuation. However, in order to sustain enthusiasm and a general 'joie de vivre,' there must be cooperation between your own different inner and outer parts, with an intuitive sense as to which part of you should be at the helm in any given moment.

Thus, you are gently and lovingly invited to use my light as HAAIAH to magnify your own so that you might harmonize your different parts, as well as seemingly conflicting factors in your inner and outer worlds. And may all these be guided by goals and values based on who you truly are: a child of light, a carrier and broadcaster of light, and a unique ray of aspiring magnificence with the potential to inspire the radiance of others.

And so dear one, bring your shining to the world, which so much needs what only you can give, so that you may increase the light of the world and the "bigger picture" of humanity which your inner Divinity is continually envisioning. Amen...

27 YERATEL

(YEH-rah-TEL)

Propagation of the Light (S)

'One who grows the light with love and truth'

Archangel ~ TZADKIEL

Leo / Jupiter (8/2-6)

I AM THAT WHICH...

helps to germinate the Divine light-seeds carried by your soul and planted in your heart in order to awaken you to your true nature and increase your personal radiance.

*Light is propagated by two active aspects: **Truth**, which represents the <u>Isness</u> of the Divine I AM that is reprised in the unique I Am of your personal Divine-Human beingness; and **Love**, that which grows and makes more of Isness, both cosmically and in all of Creation. The 'light seeds' carried by your soul into your human form hold bits of cosmic information about your eternal identity as well as your soul purposes in this lifetime. As internal and external energies help these seeds to germinate, your Divine soul-spark is ignited as a flame of love and truth in your heart that can inspire, sustain and increase you through all the opportunities and challenges of your life. As you come to realize—and value—the truth of who you are and what you love, you are better able to create a life that feels worthwhile for yourself as an embodied expression of the Divine, and for what you are thus more fully able to contribute to the lives of others. Everything about you is held in your personal energy as a field of light. This gives your presence a unique 'light-print' that emanates from you and is conveyed to others as an energetic 'hello' of welcoming (or not) before you've even said a word! As delicate and deep as the magic of your light is, the immediate effect is what you refer to as the 'vibe you give off.'*

111

Thus, your light is your calling card—it will both precede your coming and linger after your going. Every space you enter will be affected by your light—whether it be your own or someone else's home or workplace, or the space of another person's heart, mind or body. That said, it is natural in physical life that your personal light will waver from moment to moment or day to day between a bright glow and a 'sleeping ember.' For just as in the seasons of the natural world, it is the nature of light to contract and expand, wax and wane, radiate and recede—and your personal radiance will be affected not only by your internal environment and that of others in your proximity, but also by the quality of external light you are exposed to such as bright or dark surroundings, the company you keep, and both figurative and literal clear or cloudy skies. But although external light-and-shadow events and presences in the world may affect your light, you have the power to grow your light and make it visible, conscious and life-affirming for you and everyone around you through expressions and actions of love.

As the Divine light source that radiates throughout the cosmos and from within you as YERATEL, I tell you that it is love—love of self, love of each other and love for the work and purpose you bring to the world—which makes you most luminous. For it is love which reveals and grows the greater truth of you and any being or circumstance. It is love that precedes, enlivens and will outlive all dogmas, belief systems and relative truths. It is love in the soul of your being that quickens the inner codes of Divine Light that hold your unique potentials and purposes for this lifetime. By tapping the spiritual magic of your heart to cultivate love and compassion for self and others in all your being and doing, you may sprout the light-seeds shimmering in the greenhouse of your heart and shine forth the particular colors of Divine Love and Truth that you are—which can help to crack open the inner light-seeds of all you encounter!

Thus, dear one, may there be the multi-hued fulfillment of the Divine Light within, and as, your particular luminous hue-manity, knowing also when you join with like-hearted others that in the luminosity of your together-light, you will each become more. In this way the Divine is propagated and proliferated on Earth. Amen...

28 SEHEIAH

(say-HAY-ee-YAH)
Longevity (G)
'One who extends life with the creation energy of love'
Archangel ~ TZADKIEL
Leo / Mars (8/7-12)

I AM THAT WHICH...

stimulates the life-force within you with the creation energy of love to help release you from the lethargy of negative emotions and thoughts, so that light might circulate freely throughout your body and being to restore vitality, balance and health.

We cannot speak of longevity without reminding you that the inner essential part of you, your soul-light, is eternal. Soul time cannot be counted, unlike the time given to flesh and all matter until form falls away or transforms into another. In the meantime, as the clever among you have said, 'wherever you go, there you are.' You are the constant in your life, whatever and whoever comes and goes. But you, like all else, are a constant that is continually growing and evolving—in both your eternal aspects and in the temporal human attributes you have taken on like a mantle to give your soul voice, a 'leg to stand on,' and the palpable experiences of touch-taste-smell-hear-see. But of all that human life affords you, it is the spiritual and emotional activity of your heart and soul which most affects the vibrancy and resiliency of your mental and physical life.

Your emotions and a deeper feeling-connection to Spirit meet in your heart—for your heart is the bridge between the eternal (soul) and temporal (body) aspects that compose the Divine-Human being that you are. Allowing the conscious awareness of your soul, and the Spirit which sustains it, to flow freely through your heart, and then into engagement with all your human aspects, is like having a

113

continually self-rechargeable 'spiritual battery' on board—or you might say, an internal, eternal, fountain of youth .

Spiritual presence and love-and-life-affirming feeling collaborate in the vibrancy of your life. Without spiritual depth, your emotions can flounder in the shallows of casual appetites, fear and the reactivity of resentment, anger, jealousy and so on—all of which cause life-negating stress to your mind and body. But when you bring spiritual energy to your emotions, appetites deepen into true engagement, fear and worry transform into trust, anger into humility, resentment into acceptance, and jealousy gives way to the realization that there is enough for everyone each in their own way and time.

All 'e-motions' are energy-in-motion, but love is the most powerful. For love is not only an emotion, but the creation energy of life. It is love that grows the truth of who you are, and love which can extend both the quantity and quality of your days and years with its ready access to the eternal from the realms of time. It is also love which gives you the greatest longevity in the hearts and lives of others.

Therefor do I, SEHEIAH, stimulate the love within you so that the flow-energies of moisture, fire and cosmic light may circulate freely throughout your internal body and being to restore and maintain your vitality, balance and well-being. Thus you may experience the eternal wholeness of which you are part, the greater unity that your individuality contributes to, and the joy of knowing that your life is worthwhile—not only to yourself but for your fellow beings, your world and all the cosmos. Amen...

29 REIYEL

(RAY-ee-YEL)
Liberation (G)
'One who frees the love and truth of you'
Archangel ~ TZADKIEL
Leo / Sun (8/13-17)

I AM THAT WHICH...

helps to free your light from anything that holds any part of you hostage and distracted from your innermost feelings and the wisdom and expression of your true self.

In the demands and delights of life on Earth, it is easy to be preoccupied with the challenges of your outer world and the appetites and desires of your personality self. But it is your inner realm of heart and soul that gives your worldly preoccupations meaning. If you are continually focused on the outer you can become buffeted about by the ebb and flow of daily happenings and miss the opportunities they bring for greater understanding. Life is not happening TO you, but FOR you. Everything in your life is a potential gift for deepening into soul-awareness, as well as heart-and-soulful connection with others and the recognition and fulfillment of your soul purposes in all your earthly being and doing.

The discomfort of enduring life's events without deeper understanding can cause you to seek ways of 'numbing out' in order to escape a sense of powerlessness, pain or uncertainty. And while the 'usual suspects' of addictions and behavioral compulsions may temporarily dull the pain of existential longing—so can excessive preoccupation with anything. In the denial of your own depths you will likely seek quantity of people, things and experiences rather than quality. For example, a drive for more and more money or 'stuff' is often an unconscious attempt to fill an emptiness that is not

115

being filled by depth of feeling and connection, and whatever else you might need that money cannot buy. Incessant overwork can be a distraction from the lack of meaningful purpose, just as numerous shallow relationships keep you on the surface where you can't be too hurt or disappointed by the seeming vagaries of life and love. However, all the treasures of Heaven and Earth meant especially for you are in your own inner kingdom—where feeling, intuition and personal truths hold the keys to a fulfilling life and meaningful connections with others. Your soul wants to free your humanity to experience these things.

The stirrings of your soul are broadcast into your heart as intuition and personal truth, which can create a deeper resonance of feeling that transcends the tides of temporary emotion. Feelings that you suppress, intuitions you do not act on or truths you do not give credence to, hold you hostage. But if you let your feelings and intuitions guide you, the love and truth of you will be free to create the life you desire in your wildest dreams!

Perhaps you are afraid to open to your deeper feelings because of what might be 'lurking' there. But if you follow any difficult feeling to its source, you will see that at the very heart of it is the fear of being unloved and 'unbelonging.' Thus, the cure for fear is love. And this holds true for anger, jealousy, resentment, disappointment, hate, hurt, shame or whatever—because all these are emotions that result from feeling unloved and unloveable. _To be free of difficult emotions is not to distract yourself from them, but to nourish them with love_.

Thus, my light as REIYEL is within and all around you to bring love to your darkest feelings so that they might be healed and transformed. Thus you may become free to become more and more who you uniquely are in the fullest possibility of yourself. Amen...

30 OMAEL

(OH-mah-EL)
Fertility, Multiplicity (G)
'One who loves life into being'
Archangel ~ TZADKIEL
Leo / Venus (8/18-22)

I AM THAT WHICH...

helps you to be fertile at all levels of your being, that you may 'go forth and multiply' life—especially in the ways you are uniquely called to be and do according to what what you love and what is true for you.

There is no such thing as a human being who is not creative, for in the making of you in the 'image and likeness' of the Divine you are endowed with the creative nature that is a reflection and 're-enactment' of the Divine nature within your humanity. What is important to understand about your Divine-Human beingness is that you are here to express <u>particular</u> qualities of creativity unique to you in the fulfillment of your potential in this lifetime. For truly, in the commingling of your soul with the clothing of your humanity, you are a new and unique creation of the Divine on Earth.

Sometimes because of hurt and disappointment in this current lifetime or another, you may harbor unrequited desires or other impedances that can distract you from what you are here to create in this life. Or perhaps you have desires which come from a soul-sense of your totality which may not be quite ready to manifest in time. Successes can feel as if the universe is supporting your efforts and that you are on the right road. Seeming failures can make you wonder if you are going down the wrong road, or if you need to try harder, if you're being 'tested, or even perhaps if you're undeserving. But as the wise have said—there is no failure, only learning. And so,

117

we suggest that you use <u>seeming</u> 'failures' as an opportunity to examine if you really want what you are striving toward—and for right and true reasons. If so, then receive the gifts of your seemingly thwarted attempt, get creative and keep going! If not, dare to change it up!

We want you to know that you have whatever you need and whatever it takes to do what is true for you. And thus, we suggest that persevering against all odds be governed not by other people's desires for you, your own 'shoulds,' potential wealth or prestige, or sheer stubbornness—but by one criteria only: **do you love it and truly want it**?

If you love that which you are striving toward, then you must become attuned with how it wants to be birthed and what it wants to make of itself, and you must trust all the stages and timing of how it desires to come into being—including the gestation period in which its manifestation is not yet visible or evident. Just as a newly pregnant mother begins to nourish and take care of herself as the source of her baby's nourishment before she even feels a flutter of the new life within her, so must you establish a new dignity of self-love and care while you are nurturing your idea and creation into being. And while your new creation will have its own 'arms and legs' and its own will and destiny, it will be born of your heart and come to fruition because of the creation energy of love with which you bring it forth.

And so dear one, I, as OMAEL, bring my light unto you and your creations-in-the-making that you might be fertile and multiply the love and truth of you in all that you birth into being. Thus may the expression of yourself as a unique creation of the Divine on Earth honor and inspire all of life in time and eternity. Amen...

31 LECABEL

(LAY-kah-BEL)
Intellectual Talent (G)
'One who puts all the pieces together'
Archangel ~ TZADKIEL
Virgo / Mercury (8/23-28)

I AM THAT WHICH...

helps you to understand how all the inner and outer parts of yourself and your life can work together so that you might live every day with enthusiasm and a richness of feeling, thought, expression and experience.

Your intellect is one-dimensional without the intelligence of all your other parts. Thus, increasing your intellectual talent is not about how much knowledge you can accumulate or organize, but how much dexterity your mind can develop by drawing on all your other parts: the intuition and deep-seeing wisdom of your heart, the eternal resources of your soul, and your body-intelligence that instinctively draws you to what is relevant to you and your endeavors, and repels what is not.

We know that it is hard to be human—to juggle the myriad opportunities and things that your world offers and expects you to strive for, contribute to and endure—as well as what you want and expect from yourself. To participate in the dance of life with the full range of your gifts and talents, all the inner and outer parts of your soul-body-heart-mind must be engaged. You must be willing to take on life, and give to life all you are. You cannot ask any part of yourself to sit out the dance without disturbing the rhythm and balance of your steps. And this is important because you are not 'only human' in your form, but eternal in your soul-essence, and thus your every step in time reverberates also in the great cosmic dance beyond time.

The first aspect of your talent as a Divine-Human dancer is in knowing which part must lead when. Sometimes it will be your heart, sometimes your head, sometimes your feet. But whether you are guided at first by intellect, intuition, feeling, sense of soul purpose in your heart, or a gut instinct to just 'go for it'—it will take the choreography of all your parts to go the distance. And there must be a guiding rhythm.

You can learn some steps from others, you can try out different dances, and you can take the floor with a few magnificent, strange and exotic partners! But you must cultivate the talent to know how to come back to the rhythms of your own heart-and-soul-song—and how to incorporate into your dance the moves that magnify your light and to step away from those which do not.

I say to you as LECABEL, the light which illuminates the parts within your whole and the whole that guides your parts, that every day, even in this moment, the music of life is playing your song. This, your life, is your time to take the floor and showcase your unique talent as a multi-faceted Divine-Human being. Thereby you may incorporate the patterns and purposes, the flow, the magic and meaning, as well as the mechanics, that together orchestrate the beautiful choreography of your life.

So 'let's dance!' dear one, shall we? Amen...

32 VASARIAH

(vah-SAH-ree-YAH)
Clemency and Equilibrium (G)
'One who balances judgment with mercy'
Archangel ~ TZADKIEL
Virgo / Moon (8/29-9/2)

I AM THAT WHICH...

helps you to use humility, acceptance and forgiveness to navigate the vagaries of life and the unexpected events and circumstances that can disturb your balance and cause you to be out of sync with yourself.

It is common in the human condition to rail against unexpected and seemingly adverse events that occur in your life. But change, by any means, and no matter what it looks or feels like, is a necessary evolver and expander of who you are. And it always gives, sooner or later, more than it takes. Any obstacle can become an amazing opportunity, any stumbling block a stepping stone. In the meantime, yes, change, in whatever way it comes, can throw you 'off balance.' However, your most powerful internal allies for weathering, and even harnessing, 'the winds of change' are acceptance, the humility that facilitates that, and the willingness to forgive the sometimes unpredictable and chaotic nature of life that is always bringing you both complement and contrast for your learning and growth.

To accept does not mean that you condone what has happened or are resigned to the situation remaining as it is. It means you stop resisting, railing and bemoaning—and start getting creative. Acceptance brings you back to the present from whatever regrets, worries or what-ifs your imagination conjures as worst-case scenarios. The humility to accept 'what is' right now, today, this moment, readies you to see the gift of opportunity waiting in the

121

wings or around the corner—which frees the creativity of your heart and mind to use present circumstances to create something new. Acceptance levels the ground so that you can start right here, from where you are, both feet under you, to change what-is to something more desirable.

And so I, VASARIAH, say—think of life as a ski slope full of moguls. And as you travel that bumpy terrain, keep your metaphorical knees bent so that you can alter your position, deflect or detour when life seems to be putting all kinds of impedances in your way. Go ahead and make your plans, but allow them to evolve in surprising ways. Set a destination, but let the path unfold. When things seem to go akilter, come back to the present time and place and continue from here. Heighten your perspective: for despite and because of all possible trajectories for acquisition, loss, seeming success or failure, <u>you are here foremost to love, learn and grow</u>.

There is a purpose for every happening, and so, let your purposeful soul 'weigh in' so that you are not weighed down by the unexpected, but energized! Allow your heart to broaden your mind beyond reason with the inspiration and imagination that can 'make lemonade out of lemons.' When you are thrown off balance, sit down and take stock. And when you're ready to stand-walk-run again, make sure at least one of your feet is under you. Amen...

July 7—July 14

Angels 33—40

Sephira 5

GEBURAH ~ Strength & Judgment

Overlighting Archangel

CHAMAEL ~ 'Severity of God'
(Also CHAMUEL or KAMAEL)
Change, purification and clearing of karma
for stronger, loving and nurturing relationships

---

33 YEHUIAH

34 LEHAHIAH

35 CHAVAKIAH

36 MENADEL

37 ANIEL

38 HAAMIAH

39 REHAEL

40 YEIAZEL

4/23 * **7/7** * 9/19 * 12/1 * 2/9

33 YEHUIAH

(yay-HOO-ee-YAH)
Subordination to Higher Order (R)
'One who calls you to higher ground'
Archangel ~ CHAMAEL
Virgo / Uranus (9/3-7)

I AM THAT WHICH...

helps you to prioritize the different aspects of your being during times when one part of you may be called upon more than another to meet a particular life event or circumstance.

You are a Divine-Human being, and as such you are not here to be only spiritual or only physical, emotional or mental. You incarnate here to express and experience the full range of your Divine-Human 'frequencies' so that you might have a fuller experience of life, love and co-creation. The collaboration of all your parts brings contrast and movement for growth and ultimately the healing of old karmic issues so that you might be free to more fully engage with the dharma of your soul purposes.

You need all your parts to cultivate a fulfilling life: soul, with its lifeline to Spirit and unlimited eternal resources; heart, the center of your personal truth and capacity for love and compassion, as well as the bridge between your soul and mind-body; your mind, the organizational and recordkeeping center for your intellect, ideas and imagination; and body, which is the physical vehicle that is your earthly 'transportation,' giving your soul 'a leg to stand on.' In the evolving of your total beingness, there are times when you must shift power from one part of you to another whenever your health, balance, well-being, and purpose require any one aspect to be leading for a time. And thus, you are equipped to modulate high and low vibrations in any part, or the whole of your being, by what you

125

think, feel, eat, believe and do—and also by using the functions of your parts in collaboration with each other.

For example, while the physical matter of your body has a necessarily lower and thus heavier vibration than your breath, you can raise the vibration and performance of your physicality by expanding your breath and inner essence into your physicality—as well as by exposing your body to lighter and healthier foods, thoughts and feelings. Likewise, when you are mentally or emotionally stressed, physical activity and meditation or prayer can create calm and a sense of perspective and peace.

Thus, dear one, I offer my light as YEHUIAH to help you return again and again to the higher vibrations of life in your circumstances, encounters and purposes while utilizing lower (heavier) vibrations as grounding and support for living and learning. In this way, all your parts, including the physical aspects and behaviors of your human beingness, will be in service to your highest potentials. Amen...

34 LEHAHIAH

(lay-HAH-hee-YAH)
Obedience (R)
'One who amplifies inner authority'
Archangel ~ CHAMAEL
Virgo / Saturn (9/8-12)

I AM THAT WHICH...

helps you cultivate cooperation between soul-self and personality-self, and to sustain or renew commitment to the values which you hold most dear in ways that are loving, forgiving and beneficial to yourself and others.

Worldly calls to obedience—whether secular, religious, personal or professional—can be uncomfortable, perhaps invoking resistance and even resentment. But true and pure obedience is something to be offered to an authentic purposefulness in your life—not as self-subjugation or contrived penance to stave off judgment, guilt or punishment—or to purchase your belonging to any person or group. Not even to the Divine <u>as defined by any other</u>. Obedience coerced by shame, guilt or oppressive beliefs—yours or others—can become a tyranny and keep you focused on, and even imprisoned by, what you fear rather than what you love.

In true personal relationship with the Divine, you are called not to a fixed belief system but rather a dynamic personal communion and interaction with your inner Divine. The 'Divine Within,' 'God,' the 'All,' the 'Creator,' the 'Great Spirit,' or any name that a heart uses to commune with and call forth from within the I AM creation energy of Love and Truth, is found not only, or even always, in your churches and temples of wood and stone. Nor does the Divine Itself require that you believe one thing over another or you will be sinful, 'errant' or 'heretical.' It is humankind that imposes these

127

constrictions upon yourselves and each other in suspicion and fear of your human nature. But the Divine, and your own true will and way, is found most truly, personally and relevantly at the altar of your own heart—the soft, permeable place of communion and spiritual transmission between Spirit and soul, soul and body, Heaven and Earth.

While we do not wish to offend a particular belief system, we want you to know that the Divine holds you and your individual uniqueness so much more precious than your belief systems or institutional dogmas. The Divine, as Life Itself, desires for you to experience the utmost joy and freedom to express who you truly are _for the highest good of yourself and all_. However, your belief systems—personal, intellectual, religious, spiritual, familial or cultural in their origin—may at times ask you to give your inner authority to something outside of you, which you may subsequently, sooner or later, struggle with obeying.

Obedience to your elders and 'superiors' is at times in your life important for your own safety, learning and becoming, as well as for societal co-existence and work protocols. But in your inner person, as you mature in your independence and interdependence, let your obedience be more and more given to the love, compassion, kindness and generosity of the Divine within your own heart-and-soul realm, which knows your unique truth and your beauty and wants nothing more than for you to express and embody these. In learning to obey first your own inner Divine Authority as it plays out within your humanity, you may better measure the authenticity and significance of teachers, guides and allegiances in the outer world.

I invite you to receive my light as LEHAHIAH so that you might experience the joy of obedience to that which increases your authentic self. Be not afraid to reconsider your outer loyalties when they pull you toward self-betrayal or self-denial. In short, dear one, we say this: obey 'thine own true self,' that you may have something of highest value to offer and example to others. Amen...

4/25 * **7/9** * 9/21pm + 22 * 12/3 * 2/11

35 CHAVAKIAH

(chah-VAH-kee-YAH)
Reconciliation (R)
'One who resolves paradox'
Archangel ~ CHAMAEL
Virgo / Jupiter (9/13-17)

I AM THAT WHICH...

helps you to continually reconcile your Divine-Human parts with each other so that they may work in tandem for your optimum well-being, and to heal karmic issues so that you are free to cultivate the dharma of your soul purposes.

At the core of all your conflicts in life is the one between soul and body. There is much your soul can do in the cosmos without a body. But there are other things it can do only in collaboration with a physical body. Likewise, a body without a soul would simply be a pile of matter with no meaning or reason for being, and no chance of ever being anything more. Thus, it is the acceptance and reconciliation of these two aspects to each other that ultimately, but also moment to moment, determines the quality of your life experiences.

You must come to understand yourself as not 'only human,' but a Divine-Human being—an eternal consciousness clothed for awhile in time in order to manifest particular potentials and purposes of your soul on Earth. However, what often clouds your understanding of this is the pain and challenges of the physical-mental-emotional life, which can accumulate and weigh down your psyche like barnacles on a long-moored boat—what you may think of as 'karma.' But to address all this, you have been given a beautiful bridge to connect and reconcile your soul with your body.

It is your heart—the confidant of your soul and the receiver and transmitter of the Divine intelligence and power of love—that can make greater sense of all you bring to it. Because of love, your heart can understand that all your life circumstances have been gifts for your learning and becoming. By surrendering hurts and disappointments to the love, compassion and truth in your heart, they can finally be understood, reconciled and healed. Only then may you become fully available to the eternal magic of the present and any future you want to create. And then you may come to know who you are and why you came into this life.

And so I, CHAVAKIAH, invite you to always come home to your heart as your personal 'true north' in order to reconcile the seeming disparities between inner-outer, soul-body, heart-mind, self and world. For here in your heart shimmer the many 'angles' of Divine light that we are and which we shine within and through you for the fulfillment of your own greater potential. Our desire is the desire of the Divine Itself—to illuminate, amplify and reconcile the complementary truths of your Divine-Human parts, and to help you continually draw from the connective Love that holds you together 'all of a piece,' so that you might be undivided and free from inner conflict.

Thus may you come to experience yourself in life and all circumstances with the 'peace that passeth all understanding.' Amen...

36 MENADEL

(MEH-nah-DEL)
Inner/Outer Work (S)
'One who dances two worlds into one'
Archangel ~ CHAMAEL
Virgo / Mars (9/18-23)

I AM THAT WHICH...

helps you to do the inner work that illuminates and heals unresolved issues and hurts so that you might express yourself truly and fully in the outer world without hidden agendas, judgment, doubt, shame, fear or defeating attitudes.

It is very common in human life to be focused on the outer, the tangible—the things, events and people that you can experience with your 'five senses.' As naturally compelling as the tangible is, however, it only ever tells part of the story of who you are. Your own inner spiritual being is your greatest intangible resource on this earth—and it is as unlimited as your willingness to access it. It is this inner more of you that brings magic to the mundane in life, giving at times an eternal quality to the seeming restrictions of time, bringing meaning to your movements and machinations, making the impossible possible and dreams doable.

The conditions and states of your inner and outer being always affect and reflect each other, and the effects are always cumulative. This is why meditation, contemplation and prayer are so powerful, as they 'prepare a place' within for eternal spiritual energies to daily heal the effects of time and place on your whole being—and also enhance your experience of life.

Your <u>inner being</u> is composed of (1) the ephemeral stuff of your soul and its connection to Spirit, as well as your etheric body which affects and is affected by your physical body; (2) your heart that

131

receives and transmits the broadcasts of your soul through feeling, insight, intuition, personal truth and wisdom-making—as well as your connector to others in meaningful ways; and (3) the higher-mind thoughts, ideas and inspirations that come when your mind is receptive to heart-and-soul input.

Your _outer being_ is composed of (1) your physical body and its systems; (2) your personality self and its expressions through behavior, actions and interactions in work, play and relatings of all kinds; and (3) the thoughts, feelings and attitudes that are reactionary to your outer world.

Your inner and outer are often at odds—however, they are meant to work together as helpers and healers for your whole being. For example, if you are dealing with a physical illness or a catastrophic event, treating these not as an 'enemy' that you must vanquish, but as messengers bearing gifts of insight—they become your awakeners and deepeners.

On the other hand, at certain times in your life, as with sudden loss, grief or extreme stress, your inner self can feel like a looming abyss full of emotional quicksand and oncoming trains of debilitating thought! When this occurs, it can be painful to work directly and deeply with your inner self at first—but you can begin to heal by changing even the smallest things of your outer being and environment.

For example, if you are grieving a lost relationship, go places and eat foods that you did not share with that person. Change your hair, your clothing style, your home décor, perhaps even where or how you live or work. Engage in a new activity or travel, perhaps do a mind-body-spirit retreat of some kind. Commune with the natural world and its healing presences. All these things can help to reacquaint you with yourself in new ways, which many of you have already experienced. No, none of these change the initial _fact_ of the loss, but they can help to soften and ultimately heal your _feelings_ of loss. For engaging in new outer activities sends a message to your inner self that new life is waiting for you—despite, and perhaps even because of, the loss—when you're ready.

You may also work gently with your emotional and mental being by using the resources of your physical being—in working with your breath, for example. When you feel anxious, worried or hurt, you tend to clench and contract, which is a kind of resistance—an unconscious attempt to not let go of what has been or may be lost or to not let the hurt and pain get too far in. And so your breath becomes shallow, which creates more clenching and tightness. If you take deeper breaths, however, you may breathe lightness down into the pain or fear, which although at first may be itself painful, will then begin to ease and calm you. It is one of the wonders of breath and beingness that when you engage the usually 'involuntary' act of breathing as a voluntary and mindful action, healing finds a starting place within you.

I invite you to experience this. Use the gentle flow of my light coursing within you to breathe, slowly, slowly...ahhhh...as far down in as you can with each breath...down into the belly of your being, toward whatever you might be feeling, consciously or unconsciously. Your breath will find where the emotional hurt resides in your body—and though you may clench or cry in that moment, keep breathing through it slow and steady, in and out, as you feel my Angelic energy breathing with you. As we go deeper and deeper, let our commingled light-breath flow all the way into where those feelings have been hiding and holding on in your body.

And finally, like the flow of healing waters, feel the breath cleansing, calming and soothing. Feel the soft compassion of soul and Spirit opening up your breath, as you open...open...letting yourself receive...taking in this balm of spiritual comfort while you gently breathe from inner to outer, outer to inner. And as you let go of any last resistance, including any lingering judgment...soften...and sigh...the long relieving sigh of a sorrow letting go of its clench in your belly and the hold on your heart.

My MENADEL light-prescription for you especially during times of hurt or challenge is to do this 'voluntary' breathing at least once, if not several times, a day. As you do this, it can help to sway your body so that subtle energies of your physicality are triggered to loosen and flow. Allow your heart to bring forth your soul-truth

133

and its love-wisdom for the healing that is needed. Let not only your current hurt be healed, but also any old wounds that may have been festering for years now rising to the surface to be healed the rest of the way. As these new and old hurts are healed in your inner and outer, may you shine forth until you are all-of-a-piece, at peace, with nothing of you held back or left behind. Thus may you—the true and loving you—finally breathe free and unencumbered by anything seen or unseen.

So may it be, beloved, all the new days of your life. Amen...

4/27 * **7/11** * 9/24 * 12/5 * 2/13

37 ANIEL

(AH-nee-EL)
Breaking the Circle (G)
'One who lifts you out of the circle into the light'
Archangel ~ CHAMAEL
Libra / Sun (9/24-28)

I AM THAT WHICH...

helps you to break out of 'old stories' and unproductive patterns of thought, behavior and circumstances by bringing you into your heart, where your powers of feeling, insight and wisdom can heal and transform everything.

There are many ways to begin to make changes in your life— through thinking and planning, creating or finding new scenarios for living, working and playing, and so on. However, there is nothing like tapping the resources of your heart for a quantum leap into remarkable change and the ability to jump from one perspective or life-track to another when you are so called.

As we love to say again and again, your heart—the most private, tender and resilient part of you—is the meeting place between your Divine and human aspects. As such, the three 'jobs' of your heart are: (1) to <u>receive</u> from your soul the Divinely-imprinted potential and eternal resources for your soul's earthly being and doing; (2) to <u>convey</u> the potential and purposes of your soul to the rest of your parts for the enlivening, evolution and fulfillment of your humanity; and (3) to <u>digest</u> and <u>transmute</u> incoming knowledge and experience from the external world into meaning and wisdom for your life. All that said, however, the human parts of you have a mind and will of their own. While your physicality is a vehicle for your soul and its purposes, your physical form also overlays your heart and soul with the denser energies of matter and the thoughts, beliefs

135

and emotionality that react to your external world. The existential urge for 'survival' can impulse you to stake a claim on a particular patch of ground and use all your resources to protect it. Thus you may find yourself 'circling the wagons' around the same people, life scenarios, beliefs, behaviors, circumstances—and the stories you tell yourself about them—in order to keep out other worldviews or ways of living that might threaten your sense of belonging, weaken your defenses and expose, even endanger, your vulnerabilities. Put in this dimmer light, perhaps you can see how a need for sameness, familiarity and 'safety' can eclipse a true calling in your life and hold you hostage to sabotaging patterns, stifling influences and debilitating dependencies.

Because Earth life can be so challenging, even precarious, for your physical and emotional aspects, it is understandable that you would feel fear at times. But it is in your moments of fear—before they string together to become a way of life—that you have an opportunity to tap into the dissolvers of fear, which are love, self-compassion and trust. With the ever-deepening rootedness of these within you, you may enjoy the comforts of the familiar that help to make you feel more at home wherever you are, and also give you the ability to withstand, and even relish, the winds of change and new terrains. Putting trust in yourself and your own resiliency can also enable you to let go of a displaced sense of responsibility for, or a need to compel or control, the behavior or circumstances of others.

I, ANIEL, am here with and within you to help you break out of the old and reach for the unfolding bigger picture of your life. For in the rarified ethers of potential, where repetitive circles become ascending spirals into new horizons of possibility, your life story can take wing. In letting go of trying to control the external world, you can harness the power of your internal being to rewrite, edit and update your own dynamic and ever-unfolding story of living and loving—no matter what is happening 'out there.' Indeed, we cannot wait to witness the next chapter of your remarkable life! Amen...

38 HAAMIAH

(hah-AH-mee-YAH)
Ritual and Ceremony (G)
'One who enlivens the path with heart
Archangel ~ CHAMAEL
Libra / Venus (9/29-10/3)

I AM THAT WHICH...

helps you to experience life as a meaningful rite of passage by reinvigorating your personal daily routines and scenarios with heart-presence, mindfulness and a quickening into higher thought, feeling, being and doing.

There is always a pull in human life between routine and change, the mechanical and the meaningful, the mundane and the magical— essentially the outer and inner, quantity and quality aspects of life. Because the nature of physical life is often challenging, it is natural to seek comfort in certain areas so that you can get on with your daily tasks, as well as dreams and things that matter most. To that end, routines are established within familiar and facilitative scenarios that may take you along the same routes, doing the same things around the same people and places. However, while the familiar can free you to take on the unknown in other areas, it is easy to become lulled by those very routines and repetitions that make you comfortable. Thus, you must have purposeful ways of reinvigorating the depths to keep life alive in the living, the wedding sparkle in the marriage, the holy in the holiday, the vibrancy of creativity in your creations, new dawnings in your horizons, and the joy of being in your very own ever-evolving and at times surprising, life!

What is needed for this is a way to combine the same and the different, the routine and the variable, ritual and grace, ceremony

137

and serendipity, so that life is moving not only around you, but through you and with you. Take a new route to work today or try a new food or a new way of doing a mundane task, or explore something or someone new. If you have a daily meal ritual with your family, change the seating and engage discussions that have the potential to reveal new information about family members' feelings, thoughts or actions.

Think same but different, different but same: same people or task with a new approach...different people with commonality on the inside. And if you have a regular spiritual practice, explore some new perspectives, different ways of regarding the same things—or learn about someone else's tradition that is different from yours, and find points of complement, as well as sameness within your contrasts.

But especially, since there is nothing more constant in your life than the presence of yourself—think same you—new feelings. Same you—new experiences and scenarios. Same you—new friendships or new depth with old friends. Same you, same family—but with some new attitudes and approaches. Same you—with new beliefs and opinions as old truths evolve into new truths with new information and opportunities. Same but unique and ever renewable you with a new story—evolving, unfolding and vibrant, always creating and being re-created from your own within across brand new horizons of becoming.

*Therefore, dear one, my HAAMIAH light of ritual within you is not about eradicating or maintaining the status quo of the past, but invigorating your potential with the endless possibility of the present. For here, where life is all about **now**—rather than what came before or what the future may unfold—you can breathe in and harness the rarer ethers of the eternal while you are still in time. That should liven up any moment! Amen...*

39 REHAEL

(RAY-hah-EL)
Filial Submission (G)
'One who honors what was while inspiring what will be'
Archangel ~ CHAMAEL
Libra / Mercury (10/4-8)

I AM THAT WHICH...

helps you to continually submit your past to the present—as the child of learning that you were in any previous moment submits to the maturity of accumulated knowledge, experience and understanding available to you now.

As you grow into adulthood, 'filial submission' is less and less about submitting to the dictates and guidance of your parents, and more about taking on your own becoming. The present is always an opportunity for a growing up of the past, and while you will likely bring many things of your early years and experiences with you throughout your life, you do not have to be <u>bound</u> by who you once were. That is always then, this is always now. And the best thing about any moment of revisiting your past story, is to mine the pearls of wisdom gleaned from who you were then into more of who you want to be today. Thus, howevermuch the past may have 'brought you to your knees' in difficulty, disappointment or sadness, or shot you to the moon on dreams with wings and glory days—the treasure of that past is the wisdom that empowers today and a new and even deeper-higher-greater you now and going forward!

All the passages of your life give you opportunities to continually create new and more mature regenerations of yourself throughout the span and experiences of living—from gurgling and crawling to talking and walking, from mimicking and following to initiating and leading, from seeking to finding, and from feeling and thinking

139

to doing and being. Through all the generations of yourself that evolve through working, playing, living and loving, there is the common thread of the 'learning you' that is continually evolving to become the 'greater feeling, knowing, doing and being you' which creates the 'ever-wiser and more fulfilled you.' Thus with time and experience you bring more of your isness into being—expressing on Earth that part of the Divine 'I AM' that you so uniquely represent.

There may be important times in your life when you are facing a crossroads-choice, which can happen often in human life whether you are fully aware of those moments or not. But what lies at the heart of them is the call to follow your own heart and soul when the world is pulling you to do otherwise. For <u>what ultimately determines the quality of your life is how much you are willing to allow the parts of you that are subject to the vagaries of time to submit to the part of you that is eternal, where the past and future have no hold on you.</u> It is a submission of the past to the eternal present, the personality self to the soul-self, and a submission of external conditioning and temporary appetites to the abiding innermost truth of who you are.

Indeed, the inner eternal you is always supporting, instructing, inspiring, empowering, and even parenting, the temporal being that is your humanity. That said, there are also times when your soul-self must submit to the needs, desires and intelligence of your human aspects, because the unique demands and opportunities of life on Earth are best met with a co-creative Divine-Human experience. Every act of submission from one part of you to another in a spirit of acknowledgment and respect for Self is good not only for each part of you, but for the greater whole of you.

Thus, I, REHAEL, commingle my eternal light with yours so that you may continually find the way to your inner elder. As this wise eternal one watches over your entirety from within—ever loving and helping to unfold you—let every new dawn remind you that yesterday's making must ever submit to today's potential for you to express the ever-evolving more of you in your outer world. Thus will your future be born not of the past, but the ever-presence of today.

So may it be for you, dearest bringer of the Heavens to Earth. Amen...

40 YEIAZEL

(YAY-ah-ZEL)
Divine Consolation and Comfort (G)
'One who is a soft landing for your heart'
Archangel ~ CHAMAEL
Libra / Moon (10/9-13)

I AM THAT WHICH...

helps you to return to the comforting isness of the present and the inner feeling and knowing who you truly are beyond the persuasions and cacophony of the world.

When yesterday has been eclipsed by today and tomorrow is not yet to be, come unto the now-here of this moment, and be still. When the world is cold and dark, look to the light within shining as the true ever-evolving you. When life is too abrasive, relax into the soft renewal that awaits your surrender to the love inside you. When people and things are lost in time, surrender to the eternal in your heart where all that truly belongs to you ever remains. When you are weary or hurting, bathe in the fluidity of inner light that flows into your corners and crevices to heal and restore. When the world does not recognize you, come unto the truth that knows who you are and the love that sees what more of yourself you are here to bring into being. When time gives you too little of itself, lie in the arms of our foreverness and be returned to the eternal you which will outlive all the time the world could ever give or take away.

And when being human is just too hard, lie down in the quiet in-between of worlds and whisper a soft hello to the heart and soul of you that belongs to Spirit and is only 'on loan' to your beautiful vulnerable humanity—which could not even be here without the enlivening of the Divine which so loves you that It gave of Itself to reside within you, for you, even as you, during your time on Earth.

Let my comforting YEIAZEL light help you to calm your emotions so that neither desires, disappointments, nor the terrible hurts of life, drown out your greater awareness and the higher ground beckoning from every difficult situation. Come walk with me in the natural world. Breathe in the accumulated seasons of resiliency that scent the moist life force of the flora all around you. Let the forest show you how to stand with others for warmth and comfort and yet a little apart so that each may draw down the light that is needed for your unique blossoming, fruition and rebirthing. See how all the beings of nature exist to show you that life always continues on, in one form or another—and that you too may brave the storms of life and bend to the winds of change. And let the flying things remind you of your own soul-song and dreams that long to catch the wind and angle into the light to write your own Divine-Human flight-pattern across the sky of time.

Know, dearest one, that the light we Angelically are, shining within the light you are, remains with and within you always. Receive the comfort of feeling and knowing that always, in all ways, you are loved as a child of Love. And that there is nothing conceived in love or that you have given your heart to that is ever truly lost to you. Amen...

July 15—July 22

Angels 41—48

Sephira 6

TIPHARETH ~ Beauty, Harmony

Overlighting Archangel

MIKHAEL ~ 'Who is as God'
(Governs with RAPHAEL*) Power and will;
ignites strength, courage and protection for
spiritual seeking and healing

---

41 **HAHAHEL**

42 **MIKAEL**

43 **VEULIAH**

44 **YELAHIAH**

45 **SEALIAH**

46 **ARIEL**

47 **ASALIAH**

48 **MIHAEL**

* Note that the Archangel correspondences in Sephirot 6 and 8 have been interchanged throughout the centuries by different Kabbalists and schools of thought. After additional research which shows the ways in which both Archangels are active in both Sephirot, I have reversed the primary correspondences presented in the original *Birth Angels* book, but included each as co-governing.

41 HAHAHEL

(HAH-hah-HEL)
Mission (R)
'One who brings Heaven to Earth'
Archangel ~ MIKHAEL (with RAPHAEL)
Libra / Uranus (10/14-18)

I AM THAT WHICH...

helps you to realize your soul-mission to quicken and magnify the Divine qualities within your humanity so that you might contribute to the world who you more truly and fully are as a unique and vibrant Divine-Human being.

Every sense of mission for the world must start with yourself. In order to 'save the world,' you must also save yourself. For wherever you go and whatever you do, you are as a magnetic light-wand, attracting and quickening in others the energies you resonate. Love is naturally attracted to love, as pain is to pain. From the higher resonances of heart and soul, however, pain is also attracted to what will heal it, as love is attracted to what needs loving. If pain or fear has the upper hand over your heart, you will repel healing and those people, situations or perspectives that offer it. Thus, your personal mission, 'should you accept it,' is to <u>allow</u> healing for whatever muffles your truth, dulls your light and obscures the love that has the power to re-create you again and again. The world needs your truth, your love, and the light that these emanate. And when you become these things for the joy of your own beingness, you will impart them to the world simply by your luminous presence.

The mission of personal 'salvation' is about the evolution of your consciousness, which is always ongoing—for no-thing and no one in physical life exists in a static state. Even those who seem to be 'enlightened' are still evolving, still learning, like everyone else, each in their own way and time. Like a spiral continually moving in both directions between 'Heaven' (the inner/eternal) and Earth (the outer/temporal), you are 'uploading' your experiences in time to the eternal, and 'downloading' the resources of the eternal into time. Although in the ascending spiral, the underside of each next level of ascent can feel like a descent, these are often the times of transition or challenge in which you are being invited to yet another layer of healing and consciousness.

Can you imagine pursuing your dreams without the soul purpose that gives them meaning, or the heart that inspires the love and courage to reach for your personal moon against the gravity of fear or familiar ground? Know this: it is the Divinity within your humanity that enables quantum leaps and bounds into your heart-sky of infinite possibilities! For it is your soul mission to create fulfillment for the Divine through the fulfillment of your humanity.

Thus, I invite you to draw upon my light as HAHAHEL, and the light of every Angelic Aspect of the Divine Itself which attends your particular beingness in every moment and day. Thus, may you and your unique gifts be expressed with every breath of life and ray of light from the inner and other-worlds into this one.

And may you remember that of all the things you are missioned to do in life and time, the greatest is to love—first yourself—so that then you will know how to love all the rest. Amen...

5/2 * **7/16** * 9/29 * 12/10 * 2/18

42 MIKAEL

(MIH-kah-EL)
Political Authority and Order (R)
'One who helps you find your guiding light'
Archangel ~ MIKHAEL (with RAPHAEL)
Libra / Saturn (10/19-23)

I AM THAT WHICH...

helps you to become heart-centric, so that you are continually guided from a personal inner authority organized around the truths and wisdoms of your own being and what you value most.

Just as there is a universal energy that guides the cosmic order of things, so must there be a guiding force at the heart and helm of your particular humanity. Only you can decide the order of importance that things and people have for you and your life. Only you can define and make the choice to return to your personal 'true north' when the world's demands, pains and pleasures pull you far afield, because they will.

*That said, inner authority is not about ruling yourself with an 'iron hand.' You may think your truth is written in stone—but like water against stone, love's fluidity is always reshaping your truth, and you, so that you might meet what is needed in every next new moment as what is less relevant recedes. Thus, the cultivation of inner authority is about having an inner ballast of **trust** in the native intelligences of your own heart, soul, mind and body, while at the same time being responsive to the ever-changing landscape of your inner and outer realms and relationships.*

Your heart, because it has direct access to the eternal of soul and Spirit, has a more omnipotent intelligence than mind and body. That said, when your internal order is heart-centric, your mind is endowed with greater awareness and capacity—and more aligned

147

with Divine Mind. Your physical channels of circulation are more clear and vibrant, and your actions more loving, intuitive and wise.

Imagine a society or world in which outer authority may be more and more transferred to inner authority! For this to happen, there must be a <u>shared</u> value system based on the idea that for all to thrive, each must thrive—and for each to thrive, there must be an ongoing sense of responsibility for both the individual's impact on the collective, and the effects of group decisions on individuals. We do not say that this kind of equilibrium will be easy or quick in coming—but neither is it impossible.

It is my light-joy as MIKAEL to cultivate co-creation with your inner Divine that you might contribute to an eventual worldwide shift that will be more heart-governed and inclusive. Ultimately, one individual at a time, from one heart-infused generation to the next, the Earth itself will no longer be 'round'—as once it was thought to be flat. It will have taken a new symbolic shape in the universe—one that is hidden in the English letters of 'E-A-R-T-H,' by bringing its <u>end</u> around to create a <u>new beginning</u>, with the H-E-A-R-T that is needed to forge a new world, reborn unto the Love that originally created it.

So may it, and you, shapeshift into more and more of your true heart-full nature. For truly, both Earth and Heart are where Love long ago came to put down roots—and is continually doing so for the benefit of you and all as diverse expressions of Life Itself. Let love— and its handmaidens of compassion, kindness and forgiveness—be your true and constant governor, and all will be well on your Earth. Amen...

43 VEULIAH

(vay-OO-lee-YAH)

Prosperity (R)

'One who shines the love-light of possibility'

Archangel ~ MIKHAEL (with RAPHAEL)

Scorpio / Jupiter (10/24-28)

I AM THAT WHICH...

helps you to become aware of your unique wealth of inner resources, from which you may continually self-generate prosperous circumstances and outcomes.

You have remarkable qualities, the value of which cannot be measured in a fixed currency, but nevertheless can help to yield whatever you truly need or desire. Prosperity is about the flow of energy, and energy has many forms—only some of which are money and material assets, which in the greater scheme of things have a short 'shelf life.' True prosperity yields 'gifts that keep on giving:' love, intelligence, creativity, selfulness, generosity, family and friendship, the lushness of the natural world and humankind's remarkable creations of art, music, literature, architecture, mathematics, the sciences—and of course, the immeasurable treasures of Spirit that are yours to manifest on Earth.

I invite you to use my prosperity light to focus on what you want—not on the money or circumstances you think you must have in order to get it. For example, you may want to travel the world, but you have no money. However, you may have a talent such as writing, performing or assisting with certain tasks that will draw you to someone willing to sponsor you to travel the world and do your thing. Or perhaps you want to go to college, but funds are lacking—yet there are ways to go to school via organizations, grants, work-study, military service and so on that would pay the tuition of employees or members who want to get a degree. Start thinking of money as only one kind of prosperity—and the need for money as a creative challenge—and you will experience the magic of the many different kinds of prosperity that bring you experiences, relationships and opportunities that money could never in a million years afford!

I offer you the abundance of my VEULIAH-light every day upon your waking to help you create a most prosperous day of opportunities, joy, relatings, sharing, gratitude, and the offering of your inner bounty to all you meet and do. Attend to the richness within you and others, and allow prosperity to emerge between and among you as a shared light of co-creativity, care, kindness and generosity. In the flow of giving and receiving, prosperity is magnified into more than the sum of the numbers, as we too, Angelically all, add our magnitude of light to yours.

In summary, dear innately prosperous and proliferate one, open...open...open your heart, mind and soul and welcome the inpouring and outpouring so that your love cup runneth over into all parts of you and your endeavors through the days and circumstances of your wondrous and ever-increasing life. Amen...

44 YELAHIAH

(yay-LAH-hee-YAH)
Karmic Warrior (R)
'One who heals the past by loving it.'
Archangel ~ MIKHAEL (with RAPHAEL)
Scorpio / Mars (10/29-11/2)

I AM THAT WHICH...

helps you to heal hurts done to yourself or others through compassion and forgiveness—even though there may not yet be understanding.

It is almost impossible to not accumulate the 'karma' of hurt and pain in physical life because the density of vibrations in the physical can cause the forgetting of your higher nature and your internal eternal resources that are always available to support you. And so, while hurtful acts to self or others created in the life journey provide contexts for learning and growth, they must also be healed in the life journey, sooner or later. Thus you might become free to pursue your purposes and potentials in the fulfillment of yourself—and as a catalyst and inspiration to others. For ultimately <u>you must heal so that you can help—because it is the deepest desire and satisfaction of your soul to do so</u>.

At the heart of hurting is often a terrible self-judgment that one is undeserving and has therefore been disenfranchised or rejected by life and love, the world, and even by the Divine Itself. If these feelings of shame and punishment continue to be harbored rather than healed, your 'karma,' a vibratory collection of unhealed issues, will keep drawing that same experience of life—even from one lifetime to another. It sounds heavy, doesn't it? Well, it is—and the idea of having to go back into the past to analyze and figure it all out likely just adds to the weight.

As it has been said, 'hurt people hurt people.' Sometimes those who are hurt turn the pain and anger of their hurt toward others, and sometimes they turn it against themselves. Either way, the hurt gets magnified, and will continue to be unless something intervenes. To be a 'karmic warrior' is to cut through all that history of hurting so that some light can get into those dark corners of pain and coax them to the surface to be healed. But one must use the right 'sword.' And in the best case, it is not always the sharp execution of word or deed that will draw pain out into the light in a way that allows healing to begin.

Hurt sits like a hard stone in the heart, and it cannot be 'riven' by something else that is hard or resistant. Rather it must be softened by compassion and ultimately dissolved in the light of love's acceptance. Love's acceptance does not imply approval. But if all suffering is the result of resistance, then acceptance is the cure to resistance and therefore to suffering itself. Accept even without understanding. Let go of suffering over a past that could not go on. For that was then, but this moment of presence is now, where all new things and ways of being are possible. Thus, submit this moment to love, for only love wields those transformative powers.

I say to you as YELAHIAH of the Divine Itself: through love's acceptance, you will cease to be a hostage of the past and come into the eternal mystery of the present, where all your power lies to change the past by changing its effect on you. For only in the present can you conjure the eternal power of the love that softens and heals beyond the vagaries, judgments and even partial remedies, of time. Even beyond your earthly concepts of forgiveness. For the greater purpose of forgiveness is *for giving you back to yourself*.

Thus, dearest heart, may you be freed of 'what was' to move toward 'what will be' waiting in the light-wings of your willingness to be here and now in every new loving moment. Amen...

45 SEALIAH

(say-AH-lee-YAH)
Motivation and Willfulness (S)
'One who fires your heart-motor'
Archangel ~ MIKHAEL (with RAPHAEL)
Scorpio / Sun (11/3-7)

I AM THAT WHICH...

helps you to keep your motivation and will strong by drawing on the love that ignites your full and true engagement in life, and the offerings of nature that support you energetically.

The greatest personal motivator and sustainer within you is love. Even for those of you who are 'truth-seekers,' and who may think the motivation in all your endeavors is to seek truth—you likely do so because of your <u>love</u> for truth. Whether you call that love passion, obsession, enthusiasm, drive, determination, or by any other moniker, it is likely that your motivation is at the heart about love. And when you are committed to that love, you are compelled to reignite the fire again and again when other feelings and facts might deter you.

<u>You will know what you truly want by what you love</u>. There is nothing so strong as the creation energy of love, and no truth can be gathered or expressed in its full scope and strength without it. And at the same time, love also depends on truth for direction and focus. Thus, if there are times when your will to engage in something feels weak or subdued, look to what your heart is telling you before you judge yourself for hanging back. Consider if what is being asked of you by others, or by your own need to belong or fit in, goes against what your heart really wants. Let no other being determine your truth or harness your will. Let not even your personal beliefs, dogmas or belief systems, or any 'shoulds' or 'musts' be a tyranny to

your own true will. For you will not be able to harness the motivating fire of your heart and soul if your own goals, values or beliefs are not in harmony with these.

Purposes of heart and soul must also be supported by your physical aspects so that your motivation has a motor, and your motor will have the fuel your will needs to go the distance. Thus, we suggest to utilize on both physical and symbolic levels the offerings of nature, medicinal plants and the four elements: the fire that purifies and warms, the water that irrigates and washes away obstructions, the bounties of the earth that fructify and nourish, and the air which supports breath and the winds of change that disperse the seeds which perpetuate the life cycles. These, combined with sufficient rest and respite, can not only restore you but also help you to access the creative energies of the eternal realms which are continually supporting and recreating you.

Because of the vagaries of physical life and the natural movements of the cosmos, your motivation and will are likely to be affected by the energetic tides of ebb and flow that underpin all of life. But you can renew your equilibrium no matter what outer circumstances show up if you always return to the eternal 'twin-flames' of love and truth within your heart. For these are fed by the soul-spark of your inner Divine, which carries the fire of purpose that renews your will and wonder for entering into cycles of new becoming.

Thus, dear one, allow my SEALIAH-light to join yours to fire up your will to be and do, your zest for life, and the love and truth you came here to root and blossom on Earth in ways only you can. And if ever your will is hesitant, remember this, that only love can grow the truth of who you are. Any other motivation will sooner or later run out of road. Amen...

46 ARIEL

(AH-ree-EL)

Perceiver and Revealer (G)

'One who demystifies the mysteries'

Archangel ~ MIKHAEL (with RAPHAEL)

Scorpio / Venus (11/8-12)

I AM THAT WHICH...

helps you to follow the threads of your intuitions and inner truths with the all-seeing, all-knowing powers of Love in order to 'know thyself' and perceive which parts of Divine Love and Truth, Thought and Being you have come to uniquely represent, reveal and express in this life.

Because you are made 'in the image and likeness' of the Divine, what is important about discovering more of who you are is that, in so doing, you also may come to know more of the Divine Itself. For just as the cosmic patterns and purposes of the Divine are played out within your humanity, so do the qualities, desires, purposes and potentials of your humanity provide keys to the nature and desires of the Divine in its expression through you.

Every true desire you have is a reenactment of the desires of the Divine for Itself, and for you as a creation of Itself—just as with you and your own creations and offspring. For example, are not your greatest heart's desires to love and be loved, to know who you are and what more you might become, and to give something to the world from the love and truth of who you are? Do you not want the best for your children, that they might be happy in their lives and fulfilled in their own dreams and desires? These fundamental desires within you are a reprise of the Divine Itself, expressing through your humanity as 'marks of the Maker' imprinted within your very soul— which are ultimately conveyed unto your heart as personal truths, intuitions, desires and longings which motivate you into greater becoming.

Love is the great illuminator, the connective vibrational 'glue' among the threads that weave together the tapestry of your life, giving meaning and motion to all you feel, desire and do. And thus you cannot know or become yourself truly and fully without love— love of self, love of others, love of purpose and the love of life that not only embraces the 'good times,' but also allows and even welcomes the challenges and changes that stimulate ever more self-discovery and new becoming.

And so, I reveal this to you as the light of ARIEL: Whatever you seek to know about yourself, only love will show you the greater truths of who you are and what more you long to be, in both time and eternity. For it is love that unlocks the codes of the Divine Mysteries within you that are also embodied by you. Thus, in order to truly see yourself in the fullness of your Divine-Human beingness, you must use the looking glass of love to see God within you, expressing Itself through you, as you.

In addition, here is the win-win for both your Divine-Human particularity and the totality of the Divine Itself: since Love is also the creation energy of the cosmos—the more you are motivated and moved by Love, the more you are able to bring of yourself into being and expression. And thus, the more you will have magnified the presence of the Divine on Earth.

And so dear one, it is the greatest wish of all that is Divine that you might see the truth of yourself as we do—as the unique Divine-Human soulstar that you are, shining with and within us, as we shine within you, from your innermost altar of love-lit beingness. Amen...

47 ASALIAH

(ah-SAH-lee-YAH)
Contemplation (G)
'One who sees the patterns and purposes'
Archangel ~ MIKHAEL (with RAPHAEL)
Scorpio / Mercury (11/13-17)

I AM THAT WHICH...

helps to reveal the patterns of the Divine at work and play within your humanity by elevating your awareness to the 'bigger picture' of your life as a co-creation between your inner Divinity and your humanity.

You are a particular and unique constellation of Divine qualities engaged in the wonder of human experience. In moments when you are able to perceive beyond the mundane or dramatic minutia of your day, you will be able to see the universal dynamics within your own personal desires, your search for meaning and urge to create, as well as in the changes and ongoingness of your seasons and cycles. Viewing your life from an inner/higher perspective doesn't have to mean that you will be less committed or present in your practical life. Indeed you are able to be more present and engaged when you step back from the motion and emotion of events to see them in a different light of meaning and mattering.

And so, to be contemplative in your depths does not create the detachment that implies unfeeling, but the non-attachment that allows the deeper streams of your life to ebb and flow naturally without resistance. In non-attachment, you can appreciate all that occurs as the diverse expressions of energy flowing to and from, within and around you—even in scenarios of challenging contrasts.

The gift of contemplation, suggesting 'with template,' 'within the temple,' or 'the temple within,' brings the heightened awareness that *you are always pregnant with Divine potential, always giving birth to the Divine through the temple of your own being. This is because the Divine template—the 'temple' blueprint which conveys the Divine Light-Essence into sentient matter and form—is a living breathing consciousness within you that over the entire course of your life is expressing the Divine 'I AM' through, and as, your own ever-evolving personal 'I-Am.'*

This awareness will enable you to feel more and more how your desire to know and express a truer and truer self, to love and be loved and to create from the emerging truths of yourself, are all presentations of the Divine Nature expressing Itself through you, for you—and even as you.

My beloved, to be in a continual state of contemplation is to be conscious, present and purposeful in your great and small relatings, choices and actions. It is to know that you are made of God-stuff, and that together, you and every individualized particularity in all the universes represent and express the diversity and light-and-dark totality of the greater 'I AM'—and that there is no-thing or no one that does not. Understanding this brings the extraordinary light of consciousness that contemplation offers. Thereby you may know the heights and depths of who you are and delight in what more you might infinitely manifest of your own totality in the realm of time.

Thus, I, ASALIAH, invite you to live your daily life conscious of the "as above, so below" patterns of the Divine template at work and play within you. And with my temple-light may you see that everything you feel, think and do makes a ripple not only in the fabric of time and in the collective soul of your world, but in the eternal sea of consciousness. For while you contemplate the heavens, the heavens are contemplating you. So may you know. Amen...

48 MIHAEL

(MIH-hah-EL)
Fertility and Fruitfulness (G)
'One who taps the light-elixirs of life'
Archangel ~ MIKHAEL (with RAPHAEL)
Scorpio / Moon (11/18-22)

I AM THAT WHICH...

helps to harmonize inner and outer masculine and feminine energies so that all your diverse parts are working to support your whole being and potential.

Fertility of all kinds is about the collaboration of contrasts and how each uniquely contributes to the expression of the whole. Starting with an individual, if you are a woman, your outer form is likely dominantly feminine, while the masculine expresses in a complementary role as an inner energy—and the reverse if you are a man. However, the degree and proportion to which outer and inner genders are expressed, and which one becomes more dominant emotionally, mentally, physically or functionally, depends upon the purpose your unique soul expression has undertaken in your current life.

Many of you experience conflict, both internally and in the world, with gender issues and the seeming polarities of masculine (assertive) and feminine (receptive) energies and the roles expected of them. However, contrasts and polarities are not meant to be oppositional, but complementary, facilitative and mutually supportive. A simple example of this is how inspiration and creativity, which are feminine expressions of the life force, need form and function (masculine, or assertive, expression) in order to be fully manifested as tangible <u>works</u> of art, architecture, usable products of all kinds, and so on. Thus, feminine energies—which tend to be receptive, conceptual, diffuse and layered with potential, nuance and meaning—could not come into their fulfillment without the focalizing force of masculine energies. Just as the masculine energies and forms of manifestation might not have inspired or meaningful content to materialize without the creative energy and depth of the receptive feminine. Both of these energies are in play within every creator who brings into the world 'something from (a seeming) nothing.'

In whatever ways diverse energies are combined and presented to express both the inner and outer you, you must engage and utilize them in order to tap the depths of your fertility and potential. Just as a whole day is composed of both the light and the dark, so are you made whole and vital by the synergy of all your aspects—some of which are similar and some contrasting—but all of them potentially complementary if you allow them to work creatively together.

The root of duality in human life is in the first emergence of 'Other' from the Primordial One. Just as you become more of who you are by what you birth and create throughout your life, as well as by engaging with the diverse others surrounding you—so does the Divine Totality come to know what more it is by what more Its creations create and become. The Divine Urge for Creation that has brought forth the infinite rainbow of forms also resides within you, and can make the Divine, and Its creations, ever more knowable and relatable to yourself, to others, and to all the cosmos.

My light as MIHAEL is given unto you to see that it is the complement of your polarities, dualities and diversities that enables your life to multiply and increase. An opportune gift waiting to be given and received in every encounter and endeavor is to be able to engage with interest, curiosity, and even humor, the different ways life energies manifest and mingle. And so, leave off the judgments, exclusivities and resistances that negate life's infinite creativity. Allow both masculine and feminine energies to express within and among you in ways that most reflect who you and each truly are.

Thus may you thrive in the bringing forth and blossoming of yourself unto the world and each other. So may it be. Amen...

July 23—July 31

Angels 49—56

Sephira 7

NETZACH ~ Victory

Overlighting Archangel

HANIEL ~ 'Grace of God'
Joy, light, insight and true unselfish love
through relationship with the Divine

---

49 VEHUEL

50 DANIEL

51 HAHASIAH

52 IMAMIAH

53 NANAEL

54 NITHAEL

55 MEBAHIAH

56 POYEL

49 VEHUEL

(VAY-hoo-EL)
Elevation, Grandeur (R)
'One who in-spirits the magnificence of the higher'
Archangel ~ HANIEL
Sagittarius / Uranus (11/23-27)

I AM THAT WHICH...

helps you to ascend to your inner higher ground of heart and soul so that you may engage the greater powers of love and truth within you that compose who you are and what more you desire to become as a Divine-Human being.

While the word 'higher' is much used in your spiritual vocabularies to connote something ascendant, more noble than your humanity, it is important to understand that the 'higher' is not 'up or out there somewhere,' separate from or better than you. The 'higher' is within you, and you access it by drawing from your own inner eternal resources to bring more mindfulness and meaning into your thoughts, feelings, attitudes and outer being and doing. 'Higher' is a finer, less dense vibration which can bring into being and expression more of who you are.

Your inner realms are wondrous, mysterious and infinitely capable—something that your physically-finite being may have a hard time fathoming, understandably. The higher purpose of your body and mind is to stake a claim for your soul-presence on Earth in the grounding of form, time and place. 'But why?' you have asked through the eons of forgetting that the density of physical life subjects you to. 'What is the meaning and purpose of all this creation and movement of matter? Why does this matter matter to me, to us? Why am I here?'

163

These questions, both personal and universal, are best answered from within, because your within has access to everything—all knowledge, all understanding, all that exists in and beyond time. It is through your own inner realms of heart and soul that you are connected to the 'mainframe' of the universal brain, so to speak. This is more than your common understanding of a brain, of course, though your machines often mimic functions of the brain that you are rarely aware of using.

There is a tendency for the human mind to exclude or minimize what it cannot understand, which ultimately weakens its powers and perceptions. The trade-off is a seeming sense of safety in what is known and familiar. However, the exquisiteness, the magic, of life is in going beyond what you already know into the wonders of what is yet to be revealed or created. You contain the Divine template within you to do so.

The universal brain is a two-lobed commingling of Divine Heart and Mind. Together these orchestrate the Love and Truth that give meaning and movement to all of life. As the One I AM continually differentiates into the many, each manifestation becomes an I AM THAT WHICH—each one expressing unique aspects of the Totality. The right and left lobes of your own brain reprise the universal brain, but the greater powers of your mind must be unlocked by the wisdom keys of love and truth held in your heart.

Thus I, VEHUEL, am as an inner Angelic beacon beckoning you to the higher realms within you in order to fulfill your potential and realize that your existence utterly matters in both time and eternity. Together let us climb mountains in your heart and give wings to the longings of your soul. For in doing so, you will know how it feels to live a wholly Divine-Human life wherein, by the light of heart and soul combined, your physical being is ennobled and your mind empowered beyond physicality and seeming limitation.

That is what 'ascension'—or heaven—on earth is, and you don't have to wait until you no longer have a body to experience it! Amen...

50 DANIEL

(DAH-nee-EL)
Eloquence (R)
'One who uses words to bring forth life'
Archangel ~ HANIEL
Sagittarius / Saturn (11/28-12/2)

I AM THAT WHICH...

helps you to become aware of the words you say and hear, and how they affect your own feeling, being and doing, and to learn to regenerate yourself with words that say yes to life, love and joy.

If thoughts are things-in-formation, imagine what words are. Words are the abracadabras of creation, the light seeds of love and truth that have the power to bring forth new life. They are no less powerful than the Divine 'Let There Be Light,' the Logos that brought forth life from Life Itself, and the Spirit that animates body with soul. That said, words, like all things in the universe, have both their light and shadow sides. They can be used as way-showers or weapons; and they can either open you up or shut you down. Like jettisoning 'energy pebbles,' they ripple across the depths of heart and mind with the magical powers to inspire or defeat, support or crush, uplift or depress, bring joy or utter despair. In short, words have the power to propel your being and doing—or your 'un-being-and-doing.'

It is common for humans to be emotionally sensitive to what is said to you by another, or what you hear around you. However, you may be less aware of how <u>the words you say to yourself affect you</u>. Consider what words you use to describe yourself or your state of feeling or being—how you frame yourself in your own mind or the minds of others. Feelings are not facts! But every time you describe

165

yourself with some negative feeling or condition, you affirm and re-
energize the manifestation of it.

Words are magnets—what do you want to attract? If you are
tired, and you say to yourself or someone else, 'I am tired,' doesn't it
make you even more tired? Or if you occasionally call yourself stupid
(perhaps echoing what someone else once said to you), do you feel
smarter or more stupid? If you say you can't do something—does
that inspire you to try, or resign you to the seeming inability?

In addition, the words you say to or about others pass through
your own impressionable psyche on their way out. You cannot say
anything negating about something or someone else without also
diminishing something about yourself. Just as, conversely, when
you express admiration for another, instead of resentment, you
increase your own potential. Words are powerful transmitters of
energies. And so when you must call something out in the spirit of a
truth that needs to be told, we suggest that it be done with
compassion so that there may also be the possibility for change and
healing.

Thus so, as DANIEL, I am the light given to help you continually
recreate the authenticity and dignity of yourself with words that
affirm your potential to be more of who you truly are. Rather than
saying 'I'm tired,' together let us say 'it's time to get some rest to
restore my energy.' Instead of saying 'I can't do that,' let's say 'I
would rather do something else' or 'I would like to learn to do that.'
Instead of saying 'I'm stupid,' say 'that's not my current area of
expertise!' Instead of saying 'I don't believe in that,' say 'I don't quite
understand—tell me more.' Instead of describing yourself as
despairing or bereft, say 'life is giving me an opportunity to practice
trust today.'

Essentially, dear infinitely word-powerful one, we are inviting
you to use your words to say yes to life. Yes! Yes! Again and again
yes! And watch the magic happen. Amen...

51 HAHASIAH

(hah-HAH-see-YAH)
Universal Medicine (R)
'One who draws from the Oneness to heal'
Archangel ~ HANIEL
Sagittarius / Jupiter (12/3-7)

I AM THAT WHICH...

inspires you to draw from the intuition and wisdom of your heart to help discern the original cause of any distress, disturbance or disease, and to reestablish within you the harmony that is foundational to your well-being.

Most medicines in your modern world, whether prescribed or self-administered, 'legal' or 'illegal,' are used not to cure, but to manage or cover up physical, mental, emotional or spiritual pain and sickness. And even many who are not using drugs or alcohol to 'take the edge off' may be self-medicating with things like food and extreme entertainment or behavior. We know, because of our presence within and around you, how hard it is to be human—and how deeply brave you are for your choice to be so. That said, we also say that you came into this life to be as full and expressive of life as a Divine-Human being with your particular qualities, talents, gifts and potentials can infinitely be in time.

All four aspects of your being—physical, emotional, mental and spiritual—each have powers and gifts that the other parts of you don't have, thus they must collaborate together in order for you to fulfill what you came here to do. Abuse or neglect any part of you and the whole will be weakened. Physical form is a magnificent vehicle for the soul, but it is also a muffler. Physicality has such a dense vibration that it can be challenging to access the eternal healing wisdom of your soul. However, your physical being has been

167

given a bridge to your soul and the Greater Reality of Wholeness of which you are part. That bridge is your heart.

If you truly want to be healed and fully enlivened, come within. Step beyond the threshold of physicality and time into the sacred essence of heart where we dwell within you as your Angelic Divine inner 'soulmates,' always guiding you toward the greater good of both soul and body. As your inner is amplified and expanded into your outer, your soul-light invigorates and ennobles your physical form and presence, allowing you to transcend seeming limitations and be more purposeful in all your work and relatings on Earth.

When you are committed to going the distance in all your life-journeys, you will see that the 'price' of life—hurts, challenges, difficulties, vulnerabilities of all kinds—is often a portal to the prize of life, such as: aloneness to all-oneness, nowhere to now-here, responsibility to response ability, fearfulness to trust, atonement to at-onement, and so on. By using every fragmented circumstance or condition as an opportunity to create wholeness, lack may be transformed into plenitude, failure into victory and hurt into a path of healing.

Dear one, my light-medicine as HAHASIAH is given so that you might activate the great universal remedy for what ails all angels without wings, all dreaming hearts ricocheting between earth and sky, all human beingness that longs for what is often only a dimly-remembered light of soul origin and purpose. All you have to do is to say and be a loving and enthusiastic YES to your every life experience, even when it is painful. And understand that this kind of 'yes' is not about approval, resignation or defeat, but a yes that embraces all the hues of being human, and propels a first step in bringing forth new life within and around you. This is because, through the acceptance of YES, you do not use up your energy resisting what is—rather, you will be free to immediately tap into your creative power to begin to change your circumstances and outcomes to something more desired.

So dear beloved, come within and receive the transformative light-elixir of Love, which cures all things, served up in just the right strength and dosage for whatever ails you. Amen...

168

52 IMAMIAH

(ee-MAH-mee-YAH)
Expiation of Errors (R)
'One who makes whole'
Archangel ~ HANIEL
Sagittarius / Mars (12/8-12)

I AM THAT WHICH...

helps you to regard seeming 'mistakes' as scenarios for deepening self-knowledge and wisdom, as well as opportunities to start anew.

In the bigger picture of your life, there is no error or failure, only exploration and learning. When outcomes don't reflect your intentions or efforts, you may ruminate over what you might have done wrong or better. However, there is so much more than meets the eye in the mechanics and meanings of disappointed desires and endeavors, and if you are busy judging yourself or resisting whatever did or didn't happen, you will miss the gifts.

You do not come into life to get everywhere you're going 'as the crow flies.' You are not a crow! A seemingly wrong turn in the road may inconvenience you and extend the time it takes you to get to your destination—but it sets up the perfect timing for you to have an unexpected encounter or experience that may give you something needed in the unfolding of your deeper soul-agenda and the greater good of your whole being.

You don't do justice to the value of a seeming mistake unless you receive its gift. In order to become aware and present to the gift of new learning or realization, you must allow your deeper truer self to rise up out of your emotional reactions of frustration, judgment of self or others, impatience of ego and personality, and so on. Unexpected events are sometimes agents of change in your life! Seeming failure may be a lead-in to a new opportunity—or perhaps a cue to choose a different launch pad. Or your inner self asking if you really want what you think you want.

You can use a seeming mis-take as a prompt for 'take 2' or 3 or 4 or 10 in the making of this 'movie' that is your life. Even a faulty start is a chance to start again with better staging or lighting! When you accept that seeming errors <u>always</u> come bearing gifts, you are able to enter into the magic of a life in which there is no error—only opportunity for learning. Ask any creative artist about how the 'mistakes' in their creations led to some of their best work!

So dear one, my light as IMAMIAH within you is to help you look at life with the eyes of your soul to see the opportunity in every obstacle, the stepping stone in every stumbling block, the opening window next to every closing door. My joy within you is to help free you to the joy of a life in which there are no mistakes, only the more precious pearls of wisdom that come with diving more deeply into time with the eternal in tow.

These are the gifts of realization that your soul, as a particular manifestation of Spirit, is offering all the other parts of you in every present and unfolding moment of your desire—and willingness—to remember, and continue to cultivate, the more of who you are. And so may you accept and cherish the gift each time it is given. Amen...

53 NANAEL

(NAH-nah-EL)
Spiritual Communication (R)
'One who sends and receives from within'
Archangel ~ HANIEL
Sagittarius / Sun (12/13-16)

I AM THAT WHICH...

helps you to come unto your heart and hear the voices of Spirit and soul that are conveyed through the Angelic Divine via inner hearing, intuition and heart-truth, and also through worldly encounters, conversations, coincidences, signs and synchronicities that have special relevance to you and your endeavors.

Spiritual communication is the connection of consciousness between and among things and beings in this and other worlds, sometimes from within your heart, and sometimes through the outer world. It is always going on, and as you attune to a 'channel' of your choosing in any given moment, your attention will amplify it in a language you understand.

Consider that all beings are as leaves on one great Tree of Life, seemingly separate but connected through the Tree itself. Each has variations of form and function that define individualities, but also similarities on deeper levels that denote kinship and complement with the others. Every part has a purpose in the whole. Thus, every voice is both an aspect of and a unique timbre from all others. From this perspective, imagine the Tree itself as the sentient All—the Divine—God—Allah—Source—Pure Consciousness—the Great Web of Life which answers by any name your heart would call it. This great Allness is always differentiating, expressing and expanding Itself through Its myriad creations and their parts and strands,

171

waves, particles, atoms, molecules, cells, synapses, souls, faces, facets and forms.

When you are not in the body, you know all this without forgetting or straining to remember. Part of the gift of forgetting 'past' memories is to help you focus on your purposes and potentials for this particular lifetime of your soul in physicality. In this way, you may use your energies, talents and faculties for a particularized individuation and service to others—which can bring fulfillment to your soul purposes in the here and now of time and place, as well as your soul's greater, eternal life.

As a particular 'angle' of the Divine Light, I, NANAEL, help to amplify the voice of your Spirit-filled soul unto your heart. Your own heart is your most personal center of communication with the Divine that dwells within you, as you, and with the greater totality of the Divine which is the Allness of life. It is your own heart which most profoundly discerns what is resonant and relevant to you in this lifetime, because your heart is where your Divine-Human wisdom is forged to help you measure all that comes to you from the outer world against your innermost truth.

And so dear one, trust your heart, which is the confidant of your soul, your lifeline to Spirit, and the communication bridge between your soul and body. Heed your heart, always, and you will know what to do with your time and place on Earth. Amen...

5/14 * **7/29** * 10/11 * 12/22 * 3/2

54 NITHAEL

(NIT-hah-EL)

Rejuvenation and Eternal Youth (S)

'One who grows the rose of foreverness within'

Archangel ~ HANIEL

Sagittarius / Venus (12/17-21)

I AM THAT WHICH...

helps you to maintain the flow of life-force and vital life fluids throughout all your body parts, and to stimulate dispersion of your soul-light through your emotional, mental and physical parts and processes.

Flow is vital to life on every level since flow cleans, purifies and moves out old energies and substances so that the new can enter and proliferate. Water, bodily fluids and nutrients compose the medium for physical flow—whereas the generative energies of Love and Truth are the life-affirming components of spiritual flow that affect not only the vibrancy and well-being of your body, but also the healthy processing of emotions, experience, mental processes and the cultivation of wisdom. You are built to thrive; thus, when you are living 'in the flow,' abundance and rejuvenation are natural and self-regenerating. You will be more bendable than breakable, more fluid than fixed, more responsive than lethargic. You won't get 'stuck' in anything for long, because in the flow of life, 'this too shall pass.' When you are living wholeheartedly, propelled by what is true for you and what you love, you are equipped to meet life's surprises, delights and challenges with resiliency, spontaneity and creativity.

Where flow becomes blocked, stagnation can occur on emotional, mental and physical levels and may progress into dysfunction or disease. Without enough physical flow from fluids and movement, circulation can become slowed and vitality

173

weakened. Likewise, if the eternal resources of your soul are not flowing through your heart, mind and body to heal and ennoble feeling, thinking, being and doing, you are at the mercy of time's superficialities and vagaries—easily 'starved for meaning' and a seeker of 'ageless beauty' in temporary applications and procedures. Without the support of soul-fed heart and vitality of mind, the body can ultimately become lethargic and under-functioning. Because of the often dulling effects of matter and form on essence and energy, most people are experiencing at least some degree of spiritual, emotional, mental and/or physical dehydration and malnutrition. Rejuvenation and vitality must be renewed regularly, both internally and externally.

As a Divine-Human being, you carry the light-seeds of Divine Love and Truth within your soul. It is these that give your life its core vitality, for Love, as generative energy, grows the Truth of who you are into fuller beingness. To nurture potential in the inner and outer gardens of your human experience is your life work—in whatever ways and forms you choose. It is the unique blossoming of love and truth in your life that allows you to harvest what you most long for on this Earth—connection, meaning and purpose. _To love and be loved, to know who you are and why you are here, to make and give something more of yourself for your own joy and fulfillment, for your loved ones and the world—these are your rejuvenators!_

My purpose as NITHAEL is to help you continually renew your vitality by engaging with what is life-affirming for _you_. Allow me to help you to NOT 'put up' with situations that deplete you, but rather to choose life, love and truth in every moment, conversation and encounter, and in all decisions big and small. Meet the hands of time with the beat of your heart basking in the forever light of your soul. And know that as you live and love fully, the Author and Architect of life experiences co-creates life with and through you as only you can create and live it!

Thus may the commingling and co-creation of the Divine and the Human continue and increase on Earth! So be it. Amen...

55 MEBAHIAH

(may-BAH-hee-YAH)
Intellectual Lucidity (G)
'One who feeds clarity from inner and outer streams'
Archangel ~ HANIEL
Capricorn / Mercury (12/22-26)

I AM THAT WHICH...

helps you to gain clarity about who you are and what has meaning for you, so that you may process truly and rightly what comes toward you from the outer world of people, opportunities and challenges.

As humans, much of the time you are referencing life from what goes on around you while disregarding what is going on within you. This is understandable because life on Earth is interesting, compelling, challenging and demanding! Even your strong inner urges to know and express who you are can be eclipsed by the need for belonging and acceptance. 'Doing it your way' or making choices that are different from those around you can conjure feelings or fear of alienation. However—doing it your way can also give you space for cultivating inner awareness, clarity and a visionary kind of thinking that may ultimately help you to fulfill your life purposes and benefit others in ways only you can.

Understand that the light of intellectual lucidity is not as much about a 'high IQ' as it is about CLEAR thinking, whether you are weighing complex or simple ideas. The English word lucid is associated with light, brightness, clarity, sanity—and thus implies a present and shining consciousness. So what then puts a shine on your consciousness? Why are some intellects bright, awake and lively—and others rote and dull? You must have had teachers in your life of both kinds. The first likely excited and inspired creative thinking, learning and exploration of new ideas, while the second might have expected you to learn and memorize what was already there. However, clarity of thought calls both on what came before and what more can be created in the present and future.

Of course, every individual has unique interests and a unique mind and way of thinking, with different levels of engagement. What is important in your own development is to gravitate toward what makes your particular intellect sit up and smell the unfolding rose of new possibilities and ways of seeing and knowing things—ways that perhaps in that moment may be seen and known only by you. These are the kinds of moments that scientists, inventors and artists have— but so does everyone whose curiosity at one time or another is greater than the comfort, even safety, of the familiar and going along with the crowd or the status quo.

My light as MEBAHIAH illuminates for you this: <u>you cannot see what you will not see</u>. But if you truly want to see the infinite potential and possibility of an idea, situation or person—including yourself—then you must open not only your mind, but your heart. For your heart is privy to the eternal realms of soul and Spirit—and when you dip into this 'timeless-placeless' well where the Divine and Human co-exist and co-create, you will discover that all things are seeable, knowable and doable.

This, dear lit-up one, is how your intellect gets a shine-on! Amen...

56 POYEL

(poi-EL)
Fortune and Support (G)
'One who taps plenitude with gratitude'
Archangel ~ HANIEL
Capricorn / Moon (12/27-31)

I AM THAT WHICH...

helps you to continually renew a sense of abundance, gratitude and trust in knowing that you are always being supported in the cycles of ebb and flow that move your life forward.

Everything in your universe is alive, and all alive things and beings move in perpetual cycles of in and out, along with the pause, or rest, that invites you to restore and regather momentum between movements. Thus, we say, welcome not only the flow that brings you the new, but the ebb that carries away the old to make room for the new. Therefore, trust the ebbs and use their contracting energies wisely, without judging yourself or your life to be in a losing or failing situation. For just as an attitude of abundance attracts abundance, so does an attitude of lack attract lack. A sense of lack, if it persists, can lead to continuing disappointment, frustration and self-judgment, which can eventually turn into depression and listlessness, which is not natural to life. OR—you can change your circumstances by welcoming <u>both</u> ebb and flow, and trust in the nature of life to always replenish and restore itself.

The key is to step out of your reaction to observe that the comings and goings in your personal life are part of the greater movement of all life since the beginning of time. Life doesn't cast you out into misfortune or unluckiness! Life includes you in its own mysterious cycles of ebb and flow because you are in the stream of life, and you and the stream together co-create more and more life

177

by letting go of yesterday so that there is room for today and tomorrow. This ongoing co-creation of life is assured through the movements of ebb and flow/contraction and expansion/waxing and waning by which life was first birthed into being and has continued to renew itself.

The whole universe evolves by contracting, building momentum and then moving forward, though not always 'as the crow flies.' So many success stories have occurred on the back of seeming setbacks and the lessons and energies they generated for new avenues and opportunities. So when you take 'two steps forward and one step back,' consider that the back-step is there for you to glean the last little bit of insight and 'push' from where you came, in order for you to move forward with additional awareness and momentum!

For the flow of abundance and support to be continually returning to you, you must be willing to 'go with the flow,' as you say, by allowing yourself to be picked up by the currents and carried into new vistas—and also to be periodically emptied out in order to receive the new. To resist is to become a stone in the stream—too heavy to be carried forward, and eventually worn down by the erosion of time and lost momentum that leaves the heavy things behind.

And so I invite you to draw on my light as POYEL that sustains the current of Divine Love and Support through your life's ever-changing circumstances. Feel in your heart that you are always being watched over for what you truly need and want, and <u>trust</u> in this: no matter what may ever seem to recede from your life—as certain as the ocean tides, the replenishing waters of life will always come back to your shore. Amen...

August 1—August 8

Angels 57—64

Sephira 8

HOD ~ Splendor

Overlighting Archangel

RAPHAEL ~ 'Healer-God'
(Governs with MIKHAEL*) Healing,
wholeness, alchemy/transformation,
harmony, awareness.

---

57 NEMAMIAH
58 YEIALEL
59 HARAHEL
60 MITZRAEL
61 UMABEL
62 IAH-HEL
63 ANAUEL
64 MEHIEL

* Note that the Archangel correspondences in Sephirot 6 and 8 have been interchanged throughout the centuries by different Kabbalists and schools of thought. After additional research which shows the ways in which both Archangels are active in both Sephirot, I have reversed the primary correspondences presented in the original *Birth Angels* book, but included each as co-governing.

5/17 * **8/1** * 10/14 * 12/25 * 3/5

57 NEMAMIAH

(neh-MAH-mee-YAH)
Discernment (R)
'One who sees through the eyes of the heart'
Archangel ~ RAPHAEL (with MIKHAEL)
Capricorn / Uranus (1/1-5)

I AM THAT WHICH...

helps you to dissolve self-judgment, to trust in the truth and goodness of your own being, and to not take personally the short-sighted perceptions of those who cannot see you.

Discernment, like love, is not quick to judge or take offense. It studies, weighs and allows for the vagaries of time and place and the frequent discrepancies between intent and outcome that occur in the pull between soul and body and the vicissitudes of life on Earth. Discernment sees with both compassion and objectivity and does not take personally the personal issues of others which may cause hurt to yourself or another. Discernment knows how to temper judgment with mercy, too much with not enough, and how to combine and balance the needs of the self with the needs of others. And especially, discernment helps you to know that to see anything of yourself truly and rightly you must hold it up to the light in your heart which sees not only who you are now, but who you are becoming.

As you move through your world, discernment helps you to move beyond reactive thoughts and feelings to consider underlying influences and bigger picture aspects that encourage or discourage—as in 'with heart' or 'without heart.' Thus, discernment calls on not only the intelligence of your mind, the instinct of your gut and the experiences of doing—but most importantly, the deeper seeing, knowing and intuiting of your heart. And as the softer side of judgment, discernment is most wisely used in assessing what is

181

true and right for yourself or your circumstances rather than what is wrong about something or someone else. In short, <u>discernment is simply heart-wisdom</u>, which in relationship with yourself considers self-compassion and understanding to be necessary precedents to anything you can see, know or decide about yourself, or another, in a true and right way.

And also know this: you can discern that a situation or person is not appropriate for your life at any given time without making a judgment against them. There is no one on Earth who is not looked after by the Divine from within and around. Your first responsibility to yourself—and others—is that which is you and within you. The Divine Itself knows the other better than you might ever know them, and they will be looked after, just as you are, in the ways they most need.

Thus, I have given you my discerning light as NEMAMIAH to always draw upon so that you may see not only what is here, but also what is on its way to the here of today from yesterday's learning and tomorrow's potential—even as all of life is always on its way from eternity into time, and back into eternity. See yourself with the all-seeing light of the Divine. Let your self-reflections be softened by the filters of kindness and compassion so that you may come to know yourself without judgment and allow 'breathing room' for the evolution of your Divine-Human beingness.

For ultimately discernment reveals that while you are a particularity of a human seeking Self, Self is also seeking you. Likewise, in seeking God—the All—you are also an aspect of the All seeking your particular human experience.

And so, beloved, may you come unto the present with a fullness of presence, to join us, we who are the Angelic Divine as light-angles of the All, in remembering your underlying divinity, in both the light and the dark of you, the essence and the form of you—and to renew that remembering daily, and sometimes moment to moment! Amen...

58 YEIALEL

(YAY-ah-LEL)
Mental Force (R)
'One who draws from the heart to empower mind'
Archangel ~ RAPHAEL (with MIKHAEL)
Capricorn / Saturn (1/6-10)

I AM THAT WHICH...

helps to restore mental strength by healing cloudy thinking caused by confusing influences, physical maladies, extreme emotions or the overshadowing of unresolved hurts.

It is a common but mistaken notion to think that being mentally strong requires you to not struggle with feelings and emotional issues or concerns. There is no power to attract what you want in life greater than your feeling for it. But if your feelings are tied up in the suppression or denial of pain, resentment, jealousy, shame, guilt and so on—you will not have the full force—and full resources—of either your emotional or mental power to impassion your dreams and bring your goals into fruition. Feelings and emotions don't shrink or go away by suppressing them. It may be tempting at times to push down what you truly feel because of fear about what might happen if your feelings are 'out in the open.' You may think you can forget about them, but they don't forget you. They will find ways to be expressed—ways that will ultimately not let you ignore them, and may result in an inability to mentally focus or cope with life or work issues, and lead even to illness, until you address them.

In short, you can only be as strong mentally as you allow yourself to be emotionally. But you can use your mental strength and intelligence to explore your emotions and separate the 'wheat' of what is true and useful from the 'chaff' of what is not—which is anything that clouds or distracts you from the healing needed that your emotions are pointing to. Ultimately, as you clear emotional issues—especially shame, blame, self-judgment, or disappointment, which are all inner underminers—you will have more access to the deeper and higher faculties of heart such as intuition, personal truths, wisdom and co-creation with the eternal—which can then support and strengthen your mental faculties.

And thus, my light as YEIALEL is given unto you to help you discern and clear up cloudy thoughts and foggy vision caused by emotional overwhelm and unresolved issues or hurts. And so, bring your hurting or confused heart to the Divine within you, where we await, and let yourself be loved into wholeness so that the fullness of your light may be available to all parts of your being. The world needs your light. You need your light. And the Light needs your light for its own greater expansion and evolution.

And so dear one, let your heart be open, unencumbered and full so that your mind may be strong and clear. So be it. Amen...

5/19 + 20am * **8/3** * 10/16 * 12/27am * 3/7

59 HARAHEL

(HAH-rah-HEL)
Intellectual Richness (R)
'One who taps feeling and wisdom to enrich mind'
Archangel ~ RAPHAEL (with MIKHAEL)
Capricorn / Jupiter (1/11-15)

I AM THAT WHICH...

helps you to become more awake, aware and interested in the inner and outer workings and unique diversities of beings, which enables you to enjoy a heightened engagement with life.

You may have observed among you that the most interesting person in any room is usually the one who is most interest<u>ed</u>. This is because someone who is interested in life and other beings is more curious than self-conscious, more questioning than authoritative, more drawn to new horizons than protecting their small patch of ground. In short, an interested person is a co-creator of life who loves the magic of mutual discovery and emerging potential in moments of presence, conversation and co-creative engagement. How do you get to be an interested, and thus interesting, person who is the sparkle at any table for two or more? By your willingness to plumb the depths of the other, as well as reveal yourself when invited, and in so doing bring to light more of who you both are—which brings more light to both of you!

We would suggest that there are two broad 'categories' that make you as Divine-Human beings interesting, and therefore give you two ways to be interested in each other. These are (1) your differences, and (2) your sameness.

Think about it for a moment. If you are curious rather than self-conscious, intimidated or threatened by others' differences, it can be exciting and energizing to meet new and different people, doing

185

different things than you do, living in different ways. And don't you also feel a sense of connection and affirmation when you discover you have things in common as well? Aren't your books, films, television shows, social media and other kinds of entertainment also ways in which you experience all kinds of people, stories and situations that are both different from you, and also the same? Is it so much harder to be with the different close up and personal? Not if you're willing to also explore your sameness.

It is your difference and sameness to us—and your curious and adventurous nature—that also makes you infinitely interesting to us!! Unlike us, you are human—but like us you are also Divine! And we wait breathlessly to see what will interest you next, because we learn what you learn. We get to see new things in new ways through your eyes and feel feelings through your own. And we get to experience more and more of life by your expressions of love and truth in time and place in myriad ways—as well as when you have temporarily forgotten these within yourself.

Thus I, HARAHEL, invite you to tap the wide spectrum of our 72 diverse and co-creative lights to explore the rich depths of yourself and others. We wish upon you the joy of moving through your world with openness, curiosity and enthusiasm, knowing that your life is always just about to burst forth with something new! In your willingness to 'color outside the lines,' 'think outside the box,' welcome the different and unusual into your heart and mind—and navigate the seasons of life with curiosity and resiliency—you and all around you are continually enriched and ennobled! So it is and may it ever be—if you are willing. Amen...

60 MITZRAEL

(MITS-rah-EL)
Internal Reparation (R)
'One who heals the inner to repair the outer'
Archangel ~ RAPHAEL (with MIKHAEL)
Capricorn / Mars (1/16-20)

I AM THAT WHICH...

helps to transform the conditions of your life by drawing from the eternal resources of your heart for the parts of you that need healing.

If there is anything in your outer life that is not working rightly, it is likely that both cause and solution lie within—with circumstances in your outer world acting as catalysts and clues. Often the cause of disturbance or discontent is your reaction to your circumstances—especially if you feel 'trapped' between a sense of responsibility and a desire for or resistance to change. The first step toward healing, and freedom, is to become willing, which is the cure for resistance and the solution for what you desire. Accept what was and is, and you will be free to work on what could be.

If you consider that your soul is always orchestrating events and circumstances for your ultimate betterment, you will recognize negative conditions as opportunities to shape and reshape your outer world of manifestation and expression to align more closely with your inner being. Listen to your personal truths to learn who you are at present and what you need and want, and let these play in your life choices toward your ongoing becoming. Use your hurting places to show you what needs healing and to stimulate new growth within you. Regard people and circumstances that 'rub you the wrong way' as the 'sand in your oyster' that can turn you into a shiny pearl!

187

In short, welcome whatever challenge or difficulty comes your way as an awakener and agent of change. And the kind of change that is most impactful, in that it reverberates into all aspects of your life, is a change of heart. As a bridge between your inner and outer, your heart is the amplifier and communicator for your soul and its lifeline to Spirit. Your heart is also your inner truth-teller, and the place wherein your knowledge and life experiences are alchemized into wisdom. In addition, much that happens in your life is registered emotionally in your heart. Thus your heart holds the impact of your memories and whatever joys, hurts or judgments may accompany them, which may play into the story and beliefs you harbor about yourself.

And so, inner, as well as outer, repair must always involve repair of the heart. For no matter how much you may try to make yourself think or do certain things, your desires and dreams will not be able to override what you feel and believe at the core of you. Yet if you are willing to go in deeper and meet the Divine Heart with and within your own, then you may access the omnipotent eternal resources of Spirit that will heal those internal recesses.

Thus is my light as MITZRAEL given to illuminate what in your heart needs healing. And when the secrets of your heart seem to be hidden to you, let our Angelic Divine Light guide you to see your outer circumstances and relatings as mirrors of what is within. Let trust fill your empty spaces, and gratitude quicken all that is on its way to you. Sooner or later the love and truth of you will begin to flow through the cracks in your walls and dissolve the hurts that shadow your light.

And as your inner and outer come more and more together in co-creation, harmony and mutual support, dear beloved, may you come to bear the most beautiful lightness of being. So be it. Amen...

61 UMABEL

(OO-mah-BEL)
Affinity and Friendship (R)
'One who thrums the threads of interconnectedness'
Archangel ~ RAPHAEL (with MIKHAEL)
Aquarius / Sun (1/21-25)

I AM THAT WHICH...

helps you to cultivate affinity between your inner and outer being, and to tap the resources of diversity, interdependence and regeneration in the natural world as allies for a more co-creative and resilient life.

All the things and beings of nature are your teachers, with messages and energetic offerings meant to promote harmony and ongoingness at every level of your being. Through feeling, listening and attuning with earth and sky, wind and water, flora and fauna, light and dark, ebb and flow, you may partake of the wisdoms they hold for sustaining and regenerating new life within yourself again and again.

The natural world shows you how to renew and revel in your unique blossomings and becomings throughout the seasons of your life—how to put down roots for grounding as you reach for sky, how to lean into the light and draw it within to warm and nurture your innermost potential, how to bend to the winds of change and withstand the storms of time, how to draw on your inner resources when your outer seems dormant and barren, how to compost loss and endings as fodder for new beginnings, how to carry on the spirit of life and love that never leaves while you 'leaf' past forms behind, and how to rise up and give birth to the new as you draw from the light of the Heavens, which is also within you, in order to quicken new life again and again.

All you need to understand about the gifts of potential in your own nature is available in the voices of your heart and in the intelligence of life itself that shimmers in all of Creation. If you give your attention and listening, you will hear and feel your heart and the natural world speaking to you. Every language on Earth contains keys, codes and numerical correspondences that hold sacred information. For example, the English spellings of 'heart' and 'Earth' are composed of the same letters, with the 'h' of heart moving to the end to spell 'Earth.' The sacred message in this correspondence is that your heart and the Earth itself are both where love comes to put down roots.

So I, UMABEL, softly beckon you into affinity....come and let us sojourn together in the forest, among the feeling-thinking nature beings who feel you and invite you to feel and know them. Offer your presence, your listening and your friendship, and they will show you how to become one with yourself rather than conflicted and 'split down the middle' in the tempest of opposing desires and the vagaries of time. Let their interdependence with each other teach you to see the heart of the Divine in every hand reaching out for another, and the hand of the Divine reaching out from the sky of every opening heart.

For on Earth, as in your heart, the Divine puts down roots, blossoms and comes to fruition in the natural and true time for each and all, for Love's sake. Amen...

62 IAH-HEL

(EE-ah-HEL)
Desire to Know (R)
'One who calls you to the unknown'
Archangel ~ RAPHAEL (with MIKHAEL)
Aquarius / Venus (1/26-30)

I AM THAT WHICH...

helps you to move beyond your outer personality expressions to know the ever-evolving fullness of who you are through your own heart, which holds your personal truths, intuitions and soul-keys to your Divine-Human nature and purpose.

'Know thyself,' your wise ones have said throughout your ages of time. There is no one more important for you to know during your life on Earth than yourself, for by knowing yourself you may come to know others, and knowing others brings you back around to better know yourself. Furthermore, in coming to know the inner and outer workings of your own nature, you may come to know the Divine within you whose attributes are manifested and expressed through you.

There are many ways you may come to know yourself—through your own thoughts, feelings, attitudes, behaviors and actions, loves and fears, preferences and choices, relationships with your fellow beings and the world-at-large, and also by tapping systems of knowledge which present the mysteries of the Universe at play within you as clues for understanding more of your own unique and multi-faceted nature.

The more whole truth of you is likely not how you present yourself or what others see of your persona, as in the mask of your personality. Nor do the circumstances and seeming facts of your life always tell the story of the inner you, the true you. Indeed, you may spend much of your life thinking you should be someone else, someone different or better. But the key is to accept who you are in the present, which will allow space for more of who you desire to be to emerge without the doubts, shame, guilt and self-judgment that suppress your full, yet ever-evolving self.

And so, dear one, I offer you my light as IAH-HEL so that you may create some time in your day to be present and observant of your being. Offer the same gifts of curiosity to yourself as to anything or anyone else you would desire to know: love, presence and listening. Receive the love of your inner Divine so that your vulnerable parts may dare to be expressed. Listen to the different parts of yourself without judgment, because each aspect of you holds a clue to the knowing of your whole being—a knowing that will ultimately contradict any notion that you are 'only human!' A knowing that will enable you to see what particular qualities of the Divine you are here to express through your own Divine-Human being and doing.

And so it is that we say to you: to know thyself, love thyself! For only love knows—and grows—the whole and truer truth of you in and out of time. So that, beloved, you may more fully and beautifully step all the way into the world with your Divine-Human light—that the love and truth of you may be seen and known and given time and space to grow, and that you may also seek out the love and truth of others in their diverse expressions, as well as in your sameness of heart. Amen...

63 ANAUEL

(ah-NAH-oo-EL)
Perception of Unity (S)
'One who sees the One within the many'
Archangel ~ RAPHAEL (with MIKHAEL)
Aquarius / Mercury (1/31-2/4)

I AM THAT WHICH...

helps to cultivate your ability to be 'at-one' with yourself and to see how your many different inner and outer parts contribute to unity with and within yourself, as well as with your fellow beings.

The outer world often demands much from you, and every day you are likely pulled in many different directions. How often have you said or heard others talk about how they are 'being pulled this way and that,' 'feel scattered,' 'can't be everywhere at once,' 'coming apart at the seams,' and so on? In your age of 'multi-tasking' with simultaneous demanding responsibilities, seductive technologies, modern medicine's way of treating your parts as separate from the whole of you, the pull between the values of the pocket and those of the heart—it's no wonder if you feel fragmented and 'split down the middle' much of the time.

The world will always try to seduce your attention, your commerce, your preferences, choices and time through your emotions and thoughts. Instead of allowing the world to be the 'tail that wags your dog,' running you ragged chasing one thing or another, it is you who must make sense of all that is coming at you to decide exactly what you are willing to let IN you.

The only person that can put your pieces back together and give you sovereignty and wholeness of self is yourself. The self that is not reactive to the world, 'shapeshifting' to fit who you or anyone else may think you should be—but who you are and what more you want to become in your own heart of hearts. Remember what you love, keep coming back to it, and measure all the world offers you by just that. Thus, do what you truly want to do—not what you think you should do. And still, cast a discerning eye on your own dreams, goals and work to determine if they are serving **you***—the* **true** *you—or if you are subservient to them in a way that depletes and fragments your whole.*

I invite you to use my unifying light as ANAUEL to illuminate the threads that run through the tapestries of your inner and outer life, which can help to weave all your parts into wholeness in your own way and time. It is YOUR life after all, and we who dwell within and around you are here to help you experience YOU being fully YOU as no one else can be. Amen...

64 MEHIEL

(MAY-hee-EL)
Vivification (Invigorate & Enliven) (G)
'One who brings the ocean to the river'
Archangel ~ RAPHAEL (with MIKHAEL)
Aquarius / Moon (2/5-9)

I AM THAT WHICH...

helps you to be and feel fully alive by living with wholeheartedness, which can invigorate all your diverse parts for the greater vitality of your totality.

There is nothing that gives every part of you more aliveness than wholeheartedness! And conversely, there is nothing more deadening than the half-heartedness that comes with internal conflict, cross-purposes, opposing or suppressed desires and doing work you dislike. Think about how often you say or feel, 'part of me wants to do it, but another part doesn't.' We suggest to cease doing anything in your life half-heartedly. Enlist the wholehearted consent of your entire being in whatever you undertake, and you will banish the 'battle fatigue' of life and hold the keys to an ever-renewable vibrancy at your loving and enthusiastic command.

The secrets of doing this are, first, taking the words and attitudes of 'have to' and 'should' out of your vocabulary, and substituting them for 'want to' and 'will.' In the course of your life there may be situations you will be asked to meet that you don't necessarily want to be engaged in. But if they are necessary to other things and people that are important to you, then we suggest to not go 'kicking and screaming' into sacrifice. Rather, engage as a choice, because when you choose you are empowering yourself—and you are also empowering your choice with the creative potential for it to become something more than what was initially presented.

Secondly, let each part of you lead at different times, according to what is needed. For example, if you're going sky-sailing for the first time you may need your mind to research and sort information about optimum weather conditions and location for your launch site. Once there, your experience and sensory intuition will let you know just the right moment to take that leap into the wind. And when you are finally sky-born, your body intelligence and agility will angle your sail for just the right lift, the ride of your life, and an eventual safe landing.

Or let's say you're an artist or entrepreneur of some kind, and an idea comes to you from out of the blue that sets your heart afire. Perhaps your mind and 'common sense' will try to tell you it's impractical. Should you listen to your heart or your mind in that moment? What does your 'gut' say? If you listen to your heart for inspiration and your gut for impetus and the when of yay or nay, you will likely be able to take a quantum leap toward manifesting your idea. Then the ability of your mind to sort and organize new information and experience will help to take your idea the rest of the way into the world, and the heart you started with will keep you going when the going gets tough.

With choice, your willingness to engage unleashes the power of love. And there is nothing more enlivening than loving! When you love—whether the object is yourself, another person, a project, goal or creation, you are inviting your totality into maximum aliveness. For loving invigorates and engages all your parts: the feelings, intuitions and wisdoms that arise in your heart, sharpness and clarity of mind, physical energy, and an igniting of the soul-spark within you that gives it all meaning and purpose!

And so dear one I say to you as MEHIEL both lightly and profoundly—wherever you go, whatever you do—why not let love take all of you, all the way! Amen...

August 9—August 16

Angels 65—72

Sephira 9

YESOD ~ Foundation

Overlighting Archangel

GABRIEL ~ 'God is my Strength'
Guidance, vision, inspiration for faith
and connection to the Divine; vessel for
giving and receiving, creative fertility,
and the ebb and flow of life's seasons

---

65 DAMABIAH

66 MANAKEL

67 EYAEL

68 HABUHIAH

69 ROCHEL

70 JABAMIAH

71 HAIYAEL

72 MUMIAH

5/26 * **8/9** * 10/22 * 1/1 * 3/13

65 DAMABIAH

(dah-MAH-bee-YAH)
Fountain of Wisdom (R)
'One who brings the elixir of life to the vessel'
Archangel ~ GABRIEL
Aquarius / Uranus (2/10-14)

I AM THAT WHICH...

inspires you to bring your knowledge and experience into the cauldron of your heart, where they are transformed by the alchemical powers of love into a golden elixir of wisdom.

The wisdom born in your heart is a compass for your journey toward wholeness, which can uplift the consciousness not only of your entire being, but ripple out into collective humanity and even the cosmos. Many mistake knowledge for wisdom, especially when much knowledge has been acquired. But knowledge alone is only a collection of information, skimming the surface of human understanding and possibility. Your inner being seeks the wisdom of meaning and purpose, and these are created by the eternal workings of your heart and soul in time, when the spiritual resources of your heart make something more of your accumulated knowledge and experience than the sum of events and facts. Ultimately, it is from this inner well that you may draw guidance for your life and inspiration for others.

So dear Earthened soul, bring the 'raw stuff' of your thoughts, desires, knowledge, life experiences and relatings unto your heart, wherein lies the love that sees and embraces all, and let the alchemy begin! Feel how your resistance becomes acceptance, resentment becomes compassion, jealousy becomes admiration, hurt becomes forgiveness and worry turns into trust—all to yield the peace that passes understanding.

Feel that in the letting go, things will not be lost to you that truly belong with you. Feel the relief in receiving that which you do not have to fight for but which is freely given by life itself. Feel how all the tight, dark knots of fear within you become dissolved in the light-elixir of love's wisdom, which uses everything that happens to you to deepen and enrich you in understanding.

Let this be a daily ritual, this bringing of love to everything and everything to love, that all encounters and experiences in your life might yield the light of wisdom. Let your sacred heart be what it is spiritually designed for—an eternal wellspring that can continually replenish, refresh, inform and transform all your parts. Thus, your mind will become not only a knowledge-gatherer, sorter and memory-keeper—but a 'gold mind' of greater awareness and higher-consciousness. Your body will be not just a vulnerable assembly of flesh and bone—but an energetic powerhouse of physical integrity and a foundational launch pad for manifestation with ever greater purpose and potency. Your soul will not be just a distant small voice in your heart, but a lifeline to Spirit and your true nature and purpose, and an equal partner in your Divine-Human life. And your heart, the two-way bridge between your divinity and your humanity, will be not only about human love, compassion and forgiveness, but the locus of your personal truth, the transformative maker of your wisdom, and compass for a life lived truly and wholeheartedly.

In my Angelically Divine hue as DAMABIAH, I am delighted to be a catalyst for your inner wisdom quest so that all your parts may drink of your heart's soul-goldened light. And as your soul-light is increased through time and timelessness, and your wisdom-elixir returns its flow unto the Spirit-realms, we who compose the Angelic Divine shall be magnificently illuminated and increased by your transfiguration into a fully-conscious Divine-Human being. So may you be, and so you shall. Amen...

66 MANAKEL

(MAH-nah -KEL)
Knowledge of Good and Evil (R)
'One who lights a candle to cure the darkness'
Archangel ~ GABRIEL
Aquarius / Saturn (2/15-19)

I AM THAT WHICH...

helps you to choose the ways of light in order to displace the dark within and around you—and to know that the seeming dark of negative or adverse events is an opportunity to see where light and healing are needed.

To choose life is to be willing to endure and even transcend life's continual fluctuation between light and dark. While it is the <u>impersonal</u> nature of matter and the heavier vibrational density of the physical world to pull you toward unconsciousness, it is the loving and deeply <u>personal</u> nature of the eternal life force within you, expressing as you, to transform the shadows within and around you into the light of higher consciousness.

There are times when the surest way to diminish the dark is to increase your light and focus your attention on doing so. For truly, whatever you give your attention to expands. However, there are other times when exploring the shadows shows you where and how healing is needed. And if you use this information to bring difficult things 'to light' where they can be healed—rather than judging yourself or wallowing in shame and guilt—then you have used the dark as an ally, and it will not have a lasting hold on you.

To know the nature of something is to have power over it, and so we tell you this about the nature of 'evil.' As implied by the English word 'evil,' which spells 'live' backwards, evil is living life with your back to the light. If you understand that all is One and there is

201

nothing that is not part of the One, whatever its other-seeming, then you may begin to realize that darkness as evil is an inverted, or reverse, potential of the diversities of light that express the One. And thus, it is also a contrasting energy that can impulse humanity to increase the presence of light.

Here is a basic principle of life: all created things and beings express polarities as contrast in order to stimulate growth and evolution. It is when either polarity runs amuck or is over-identified with and clung to that distortions can occur. Engaging with prolonged contracted or impeding energies can build into life-negating conditions or acts that may be viewed as 'evil.' Likewise, while 'good' is an expression of expanding life-affirming energy, unchecked it can create dilution and depletion.

We invite you to free yourself from any yoke of thinking that would hold you hostage to life-negating energies. But rather than doing battle with them, use negative energies to reveal underlying issues and inner or outer conflicts that need healing so that you might become more and more free to allow your light to shine.

Consider photography: when a negative is exposed to the right developing solution, the positive light-filled image is revealed. Likewise, however negative a person or event may seem, the 'right developing solution' is the alchemical mix of love and compassion that is formulated at the grail-altar of the heart, which always reveals the greater truth of a situation or being.

Dear ones, we invite you to trust that it is the nature of all of life to sooner or later go toward the light. Whatever you may choose or be subjected to in your life, you have the power within you to transform any circumstance into an experience that is light-yielding. In the meantime, do not rue the shadows, because they have their own gifts. The sooner you see what they are offering, the sooner they will concede to the light. That is what I, MANAKEL, am here with and within you to help you do. The choosing must be yours, but dear one, the power is ours together from within you. Amen...

67 EYAEL

(AY-yah -EL)
Transformation to the Sublime (R)
'One who illumines the inner star'
Archangel ~ GABRIEL
Pisces / Jupiter (2/20-24)

I AM THAT WHICH...

streams the light of Divine consciousness into the denser energies of your being in order to ennoble, lighten and lift your inner and outer life of thoughts, feelings, circumstances, events and relatings.

You may sometimes feel 'torn between two worlds,' pulled by heart and soul toward the inner realms of feeling, contemplation, creativity, potential and higher beingness, or by body and mind to goal-oriented thought, action, manifestation, responsibility and the challenges of your outer world. Unlike the seed which floats on the wind to put down roots wherever it lands, your soul willfully came to Earth to inhabit and align with your specific human form in order to fulfill its purposes for being here. And your physical humus, which has its own 'body-intelligence,' agreed to take it in, and on—more or less—meaning that in the compelling and seductive world of the physical, sometimes preoccupation with your outer reality resists or is at odds with your inner calling. Even so, as a Divine-Human being, both the inner and outer worlds compose your domain.

What is so very sacred about physical life is that your soul is thereby given the opportunity to explore and engage in a spectrum of experiences that are possible only on Earth in the context of form, time and place. Having a physical body gives your soul a vehicle with which to move through life, while the heart and soul within your physicality gives depth of purpose, meaning—and greater energetic reach—to the movement, mind and matter of your existence.

Your dual soul/body nature sets the stage for taking your human experience 'up a notch' by inviting the sublime to collaborate with and ennoble the mundane as you allow more quality into the quantities of your doing. Since you have the Divine 'on tap' in the well of your own soul, you can 'supercharge' your earthly experiences with the wisdom and greater-seeing that your inner eternal resources can bring to you at any moment in time.

If you are experiencing your life as mundane, then you are likely not living your life with all your parts engaged. Seeing yourself, and life, through the angelic lens of sublime possibility will show you that if you want your life to be more interesting, then you must become more interest*ed*! If you are bored with your job, a relationship, or even your own existence, perhaps you have barely skimmed the surface of what is possible. If that is the case, then we invite you to dive deeper in and higher up before walking away!

When there are dreaded chores waiting, bring to them willingness and enthusiasm—and the joy of organizing and bringing harmony to your surroundings. If you are not enjoying your work life, explore what you might do to make it more interesting through creativity and greater engagement. And if it is not enough to change *how* you do what you do, claim your right to change *what* you do and/or where you do it to something that is more love-and-life-affirming for you. The choice is always yours, even when you seem to be 'between a rock and a hard place.' Know this: we of the Divine deeply respect your will, and your choices. Thus, take one step, and the universe will meet you with the next.

My light as EYAEL is given so that you might heighten your experiences of feeling, thinking, being and doing in both the bigger picture and small details of your life. As your inner being becomes more engaged in your outer doing, the more ennobled and vibrant the entirety of your life experience can become. And we, your Angelic inner soulmates, do so love to experience that with you, through you and as you! Amen...

68 HABUHIAH

(hah-BOO-hee-YAH)
Healing (R)
'One who loves hurt into healing'
Archangel ~ GABRIEL
Pisces / Mars (2/25-29)

I AM THAT WHICH...

helps you to use the powers of self-compassion and love to heal hurts, imbalances and disease within you as if you are born anew—not as a survivor of past difficulty, but rather as a transformed person with a clean slate and a new story who no longer needs the past as a reference point.

Transformative healing happens in the heart, where your Divine and Human aspects meet to amplify the healing energies of love that are ever-present in your being. It is love that transmutes the consuming fires of self-condemnation into the life-giving warmth of compassion—love that transforms a flood of fearful emotions into an elixir that quenches and rejuvenates—love that calms the winds of change into the breath of life—love that softens and re-forms the fragility of your earthen parts into a nurturing foundation that supports health and wholeness.

So dear one, Let There Be Love.

In the mysteries of time and eternity, love is not something you don't have or must go out and get. Love is what formed you, and Love is the creation energy of life which sustains you, and which grows the I-Am of you that is born of the Divine I AM that dwells within you. This love that created and continues to evolve the universes and all of life is the same love that breathes new life into your being in every moment of your every day.

In becoming conscious of the love that you are, you may joyfully and gratefully draw upon the nature of yourself as love for whatever you need or desire. And wherever in yourself you may be hurting, do not fight the hurt, but expand the breath of love in that place so that the hurting part may be reminded that it too is love, showing you where healing is needed.

And so I, HABUHIAH, as the healing light of love, also say this to you: bring compassion unto yourself. Be and do only what you have the capacity for at any given moment, and leave the rest for later today, tomorrow, a future time—or for someone else, even the Divine Itself. If you are vulnerable now, do not suffer people and situations that weaken you. If you would be comforted, be in the company of a gentle soul. If you are unsteady, be with one whose heart is a soft landing. And if you would be healed, receive from the Angelic Divine within you the presence and power of love, which is the architect and foundation of your wholeness and well-being.

And so it shall be. Amen...

69 ROCHEL

(roh-SHEL)
Restitution (R)
'One who brings back your lost parts'
Archangel ~ GABRIEL
Pisces / Sun (3/1-5)

I AM THAT WHICH...

helps you to heal a sense of loss or of 'something missing' by first restoring connection to any parts of your being which are not being included in your life doings and decisions.

Restitution, in relatings with others, is about restoring, either literally or through 'atonement' or compensation of some kind, what seems to have been lost. In relationship with yourself, something that may seem to be missing in your life must first be found within you, perhaps just below your conscious awareness, that may be overlooked and under-utilized. Life does not withhold or take things away from you unless on a soul level you have chosen that for deeper learning. And nothing outside of you has any true power over you unless you have given it that power. Furthermore, nothing is ever lost that truly belongs to you—only perhaps forgotten or dimmed in your awareness for a time. The sense of 'something missing' that is most common to human beingness is caused by a lack of meaning in the matter you are engaged with, as when your inner self is not being expressed in your outer reality. When the truth of who you are and what you love is not expressed in the way you live your life—the choices and alliances you make, the work you do, and so on—what is likely missing in your life is **part or parts of the greater, truer you**.

It is not easy to be human, and when certain parts of you get hurt, there can be an instinctive impulse to withdraw that part from *exposure. You are more vulnerable when some part of you is hurt, so the withdrawal is partly about protection and partly about the need for healing. But hurts can't heal all the way if they remain hidden, and after a time that part of you can close off and seem to be lost. This happens especially when your heart is hurt. Or sometimes parts of you recede for fear of being shamed or shunned by others for such things as ignorance or brilliance, beauty or boldness, being 'odd,' 'weird,' 'too intense,' 'too much,' or any number of ways you might seem to be different, less or more than those around you. Alas, these kinds of wounds most commonly happen when you are in your young years, still forming your individuality while also trying to find a way and place of belonging among your peers. But in order to live a full and fulfilling life, these things must be healed. <u>For having all you want in life starts with being all you are.</u>*

So dear one, draw on my light as ROCHEL when you feel you have lost sight of your own light and the more fulfilled experience of living that you know deep down you should be having. Let us work together to heal the wounds of your personality-self so that you can let your humanity come forward fully in expression with your soul. As the restorative light of the Divine Itself, I will help you explore subconscious clues in your dreams, intuitions, feelings and outer coincidences for the parts of you that seem to be missing. As you let your feelings come to the surface—especially the hurt ones, we will follow them like breadcrumbs to the wounds that are still festering. Together we will clean and clear them with love and compassion so that no part of you will be held back from this life. And then you will let the Love that made you keep making even more of you!

In these ways your Divine and Human parts may return to 'at-onement,' and the wholeness that is your birthright may be restored. Amen...

70 JABAMIAH

(yah-BAH-mee-YAH)
Alchemy (Transformation) (R)
'One who turns base mettle into gold'
Archangel ~ GABRIEL
Pisces / Venus (3/6-10)

I AM THAT WHICH...

helps you to embrace both small and profound changes in your thoughts and feelings, which are the seeds of all your conditions and circumstances, and to accept change as your soul's way of bringing more of your totality into expression and fulfillment.

We know change is often feared in Earth-life, and we have utmost compassion for your desire to create stability in your uncertain world. However, change is a catalyst for learning and growth and ensures the ongoing evolution of your heart, mind, body and soul through the seasons, cycles and generations of your life. <u>If you can regard all change as for the better, no matter what challenges it may bring, you will reap the gifts and opportunities in everything that occurs.</u>

How you experience change is directly correspondent with how much you resist or embrace it. When pressure and discomfort build from being 'stuck between a rock and a hard place' for an extended period of time, eventually life will provide you one or more ways out of your situation. Pain and suffering often forces change, or forces you to accept change since it is human nature to want to end the pain. If you accept the invitation to change, then you may, as you say, not only 'turn over a new leaf,' but grow a whole new tree! And this is because—whether you recognize it at the time or not—the energy behind all change is the creation energy of Love, working to bring more of who you are into being and expression.

209

When you understand Love as an 'alchemical agent' of change, you will realize that Life Itself is 'on your side,' and that the spiritual energies of Love draw from the eternal to alter the very chemistries of the physical, emotional and mental landscape of your life. Love's change can turn endings into new beginnings, brokenness into greater strengths, dark nights of the soul into brave new dawns and dreams of the heart, and every difficult day into a stronger tomorrow. As Love's change moves mountains of fear, pain, doubt or shame that stand between you and your wildest dreams of becoming, you are born anew. In the presence of Love, leaden and life-negating thoughts, feelings and conditions which eat your vitality are transformed into a joy-filled lightness of being, self-acceptance and joy—even while you are striving to bring more of who you are, more of who you desire to become, into the world.

You come into this world as a Divine-Human being—a soul outfitted with body, heart and mind. Whatever the details of your particular dreams and goals, whatever professional monikers you may seek in your purpose and work—you are essentially here in physical life to transform more and more of your human substance into the Divine 'image and likeness' that is carried within your soul.

It may take a moment or a lifetime for the light of new becoming to travel from soul and heart to mind, body and the belly of your beingness. But always know this—even if you do not feel us at times: because of the great love with which the Divine has wrought your every cell as a living, breathing aspect of Itself, you undertake this grand and courageous journey of ongoing transformation in the company of Angels.

Thus is my transformative light as JABAMIAH blessed to gather your Angelic light-mates within and around you all your livelong life. By the love and desire in your heart that quickens us, we attend you as the grace of every transformative moment in your soul's precious lifestream! So it is and ever will be. Amen...

71 HAIYAEL

(HAH-ee-yah-EL)
Divine Warrior & Weaponry (R)
'One who wins the battle that cannot be fought'
Archangel ~ GABRIEL
Pisces / Mercury (3/11-15)

I AM THAT WHICH...

helps to forge within you the shield of self-love and the sword of personal truth so that you might 'separate the wheat' of your true self from the 'chaff' of a false or confused sense of self.

In your early years as a child, you learned to navigate your world by watching and copying others. As you delightedly moved about and began to discover and exercise your autonomy, you explored ways of interfacing with the world by 'trying on' different personalities and potentialities. While much early learning comes through imitating the actions of those around you, you are inwardly 'hard-wired' to ultimately seek, express and grow your own identity. Many of you have an especially difficult time between childhood and adulthood when the need to individuate and explore the uniqueness of yourself is crossed with the need to belong and be included by your peers—which means that your inner urge for individuation can be challenged by both an inner and outer pressure to conform. Indeed, it is from this vulnerable time in your life that any pain of unbelonging can linger for years, compromising your interactions with others and creating an ongoing insecurity about being 'enough' as who you are.

The time of adolescence is an important first gauntlet in your lifelong journey of learning to express the truth of yourself through what, who and how you love. There is no real satisfaction or security in belonging to any place or people if you have to purchase that

211

belonging by being who you are not. Conversely, it is your willingness to be who you truly are and to contribute your particular talents, intelligences and gifts to the world that will naturally attract the 'right' others to you—at any stage of your life. For you are here in your human life to experience yourself and life through your individuality and in relationships that recognize and support the cultivation and expression of your true ever-evolving self.

As any true warrior knows, there is no need to fight that which would diminish you if you cannot be diminished. Both those who do and do not see you provide opportunities, each in their own ways, to see yourself more clearly. Life is a battle only if you are fighting with yourself. And if 'all the world is a stage,' then life is the time and place to play yourself as no other could. If you don't, there will be a hole in the whole of creation where you might have truly and fully been. So bring your all and take your place in the light!

And so I, HAIYAEL, shall amplify my particular 'angle' of Divine Light within you to help you distinguish between who you truly are from who you or another might think you should be. Sing your one-of-a-kind soul-song and allow the love and truth of yourself to be visible and even inspiring unto others. Soar into the higher sky of your heart to paint the colors of your soul purpose for all the world to see, and I, HAIYAEL, shall be soaring with you.

Because—be cause, dear one—the world is waiting for the brilliant, multi-hued light of your Divinely-endowed hue-manity! Amen...

72 MUMIAH

(MOO-mee-YAH)
Endings and Rebirth (R)
'One who uses endings to begin again'
Archangel ~ GABRIEL
Pisces / Moon (3/16-20)

I AM THAT WHICH...

helps you to savor what has come to fruition and bask in the last sparkling flavors of the 'now' as it fades into yesterday and leaves behind the gifts of experience and awareness to prepare the way for the new now of tomorrow.

Life asks this of you: to embrace the ebb and flow of things and beings with the faith of knowing that forms fade so that the essence which remains may express itself in new ways. Revel in every last little bit of anything or anyone that graces your life, because whether you realize it fully yet or not, 'what was' has served you well! Let the seeds from the eaten fruit of your experience take root in the fertile loam of a new awareness. For every new now is but a season in the wholeness of your time here, and there are seasons and fruits yet to come. As 'the bloom fades from the rose' of every experience, learnings are plucked and new ideas and potentialities are already being seeded and nurtured in the infinite fields of your all-season heart.

Every ending carries the seed-energies for rebirth and new life. Thus 'leaf the past behind,' and let yourself be carried by the winds of change into your next new field of endeavor and expression. As you take root again, welcome the gestation times when outer manifestation subsides to supply energies for inner growth. And in the meantime, our Angelic 'light-incubator' will help you to be at peace with what-was and creatively nurture what-is until what-will-be is ready to emerge.

In relatings with others, we can help to illuminate truths that need to be told between yourself and the other so that difficult dynamics can be ended and the way prepared for something new between you. Or in a parting of ways, as the departing of a friend or loved one physically or emotionally, we can plant light-seeds of healing and acceptance that will sprout tender new growth when the soil of your heart is ready to receive.

And so dear one, consider this: measure your life not by love won or lost, but how love has brought the truths of you into greater beingness and expression.

I, MUMIAH, and all your Angelic light-mates come to amplify from within you the self-love that can transform loss or emptiness into wisdom and a new sense of anticipation. For whatever forms may fall away, you are rooted in the eternal truth of your soul-essence, which will always create new life from within you. And so, in all endings be grateful for the forms that were and feel within you the essence that is never lost, neither in the universe nor in the willing heart of you that shall bring forth new variations of the timeless gifts that remain. And so now, dear one, get ready to welcome the new! Amen...

———————————————

Sephira 10

MALKUTH (SHEKINAH)

Relates to the Kingdom of Creation

and the Realm of Saints and Ascended Souls

Overlighting Archangels

SANDALPHON and METATRON

These two Archangels, sometimes referred to as "spiritual brothers," are arguably said to be the only two Archangels who were once human and taken up to the heavens without having experienced human death: METATRON was Enoch, and SANDALPHON was Elijah. Metatron's unmanifested creation energies in KETHER are finally manifest in MALKUTH and the SHEKINAH (feminine aspect of the Divine) which gives birth to Earth. Thus here METATRON is the link between the Divine and all of humanity, while SANDALPHON is the overlighting Archangel of the Earth and planetary "caretaker" who roots Divine Love within humanity and the natural world in order to cultivate higher consciousness on Earth.

In the Tree of Life symbology, Sephira 10 is a "bridge" realm leading from the Angelic Heavens to the realm of saints and ascended souls, and ultimately to Earth. Therefore, there are no Angels (except the Archangels) correspondent to this last Sephira of the Tree. However, it is included here in order to complete the spiritual descent of the Heavenly Tree of Life unto Earth as it takes root and branches out into, within and among the hearts of all humanity.

Amen...Amen...Amen

Appendix I
Your Personal Birth Angels

The ageless wisdoms reveal that our souls come to Earth for many lifetimes in order to root the "light-stuff" of the heavens in the humus of Earth, and proliferate the diverse aspects of the Divine in the being and doing of human life. Because our soul-memory recedes as we become deeply encased and engaged with form and matter, we tend to forget our Divine nature and the eternal resources that are always available to us from within. Thus, throughout our lives, we accumulate residue from hurts done to ourselves or others, unresolved issues and potentials unrealized. These things, along with whatever our souls incarnate with, compose our "karma," and provide a kind of map for the healing work we must do in order to become free to undertake the "dharma" of our soul purposes. The 72 Angels, and our personal Birth Angels, are powerful transformative tools in this work.

The Astrology Angle. Medieval Kabbalists working with the 72 Angels corresponded their periods of governing to 360 degrees of the Zodiac, listed at the end of this Appendix. While each degree would ideally be correspondent to one day, we live in a 365+-day solar year. Research of ancient calendars indicates that some early civilizations adhered to a lunar calendar of approximately 30 days per month x 12 months = 360 days (the Babylonians and Mayans, for example). However, Earth's orbit around the sun is elliptical—not a perfect circle— and thus every few years they would tack on an extra month to make up the difference between lunar and solar cycles. In 45 B.C., the Julian solar calendar was established, which took us to a 365.25-day year, with a "leap" year every four years. This was reformed by the slightly more accurate Gregorian calendar in 1582. Isaac Newton surmised in 1728 that the original 360-degree Zodiac was attributed to the early widespread use of the 360-day calendar. (www.360dayyear.com and www.en.wikipedia.org/wiki/Julian_calendar)

During later centuries of Kabbalistic work with the 72 Angels carried on by descendants of those Jewish rabbis, mystics and scholars who escaped the persecution of the Spanish Inquisition in 1492, dates and times of particular Angelic influences were corresponded to the Zodiacal degrees, with some overlapping of dates to account for the degrees/days discrepancies. In my work I use the correspondences of days rather than degrees because they are more universally accessible, but the degree correspondences are included as the last chart in this chapter for those who want to enhance their work with astrology.

Because of the density and forgetfulness of Earth-life, it is said that in our pre-birth soul-choice of circumstances for each lifetime we also choose a day and time of birth that will benefit us with certain influences, guides and cosmic aspects to act as symbols and "signatures" to remind us who we are and support us with what we come here to do. Astrologers since ancient times have understood that according to the moment of our birth, the constellations in the heavens mirror and can energetically support the constellations of potential within the qualities and purposes of our human beingness. Likewise, medieval Kabbalists associated the 72 Angels to human life through their hierarchies of relationship with the cosmos and Creation. These scholars and mystics understood that just as each of us represent a micro-expression of the entire Zodiac, a hologram of all 72 Angels are "imprinted" within us as the whole spectrum of Divine Light-Stuff available to us.

The Roles of Your Personal Birth Angels. It is said that we are also especially attended by a particular constellation of at least three Angelic Energies which represent aspects of the Divine Light that were prevailing at our time and day of birth. Because of the body's soul-forgetting, we often spend our entire lives trying to figure out who we are and what our purpose is. Our Birth Angels help us to know and be more of who we are by showing us which particular aspects of the Divine we are here on Earth to express and cultivate through our humanity. By working within us to quicken and amplify the soul-spark of our particular Divine-Human beingness, our Birth Angels help us to meet our challenges, heal unresolved issues and carry out our unique purposes and potentials during our time on Earth.

You can discover your Birth Angels by corresponding your day and time of birth to the Angels' days and times of governing and support. Find your Incarnation and Intellect Angels in the charts below, and your Heart Angel from the list of dates above each Daily Wisdom. (A downloadable or laminated **72 Angels Days & Hours of Support Chart** is available at www.72BirthAngels.com for easy reference to anyone's Birth Angels with date and time of birth.) Note that because of the fluctuations of correspondences between 360 degrees and 365+ days, if your day and time of birth are close to the "cusp" day or time of the Angelic Energy before or after yours, you may want to work with that Energy as well, or whichever has the strongest resonance for you.

Our Birth Angels work with the physical, emotional and mental aspects of our being in these ways:

Your **Incarnation Angel** ~ Expresses particular qualities of the Divine Being and Will through your own unique physical existence, personal will and life purpose. Your Incarnation Angel is the one whose five-day period of governing corresponds to the five-day period around your birth and supports the qualities, challenges and expressions of your physical being and the will to carry out your soul purposes in your human lifetime. Some refer to this Angel as your "Guardian Angel." However, your Incarnation Angel is not just acting as a guardian, but as a support and amplifier of your particular "image and likeness" to the Divine Itself, and the cultivation of your own true will as the Will of the Divine for you to be and increase who you truly are. Thus, your personal Divine-Human "I Am" roots particular aspects of the Divine I AM in the physical realm of time and place as you blossom and bear fruit through your own creations and soul purposes.

Your **Heart Angel** ~ Expresses particular qualities of Divine Love and Truth through the feelings and wisdoms of your heart. Your Heart Angel is the one who was governing on your actual day of birth and who corresponds to your unique emotional qualities, challenges and potentials and supports the cultivation of intuition, personal truth, wisdom, love and compassion for yourself and others.

Your **Intellect Angel** ~ Expresses particular qualities of Divine Mind through the unique thought constructs and creations of your human intelligence. Your Intellect Angel is the one who was governing during your time of birth (within 20 minutes), and who throughout your life supports your particular mental qualities, challenges and potentials, and the cultivation of greater awareness and higher-mind. Those born at a cusp time (on the hour or 20 minutes before or after) may be said to have two Intellect Angels (for a total of four Birth Angels).

Angel-Human dynamics. It is important in working with the 72 Angels to remember that they represent specific, differentiated aspects of the Divine Light which already exist within and among us. Therefore, when we "call on" or invoke an Angel, we do not do so as if it is separate from, or above, us. Rather, we call the Angel forth from *within* us, which increases our awareness and engagement with it, amplifying Its particular energetic qualities in the quantum field within and around us.

The 72 Angels are here within and among us to support us and amplify the Divinity within our humanity. While they are sometimes spoken of as "governing" particular days and times, as well as the different planes of human existence (physical, emotional and mental), what is meant by governing is *influence*, *correspondence* and *support*. Ideally, because of our Divinely-endowed birthright of free will, we humans are meant to govern ourselves. The Angels, thus, do not literally govern us, but amplify the inner Divine energies that support our highest good—which is to allow love to grow the "I-Am" truth of who we each uniquely are and support the fruition of our soul purposes and potentials in both time and eternity.

The 72 Angels' Days of Incarnation Support

Most spiritual traditions understand that the human soul precedes and survives physical life. To "incarnate" means to bring Spirit/soul essence into form, which in the case of human beings is about commingling the gossamer soul-light of Divine Energy with the heavier, denser light of physicality. In the 72 Angels tradition, an Angel's expression in the Incarnation (physical) plane supports particular aspects of the Divine Being and Will in human physical existence, personal will and life purpose—essentially supporting your being and reason for being.

Thus, your Incarnation Angel is the one whose five days of Incarnation support correspond to the five-day period around your birth, and how you use your will, as both <u>willfulness</u> and <u>willingness</u>, to create more of yourself with the unique qualities, challenges, potentials and purposes of your being on the physical plane. Furthermore, the more you fulfill your personal love, truths, will and purposes, the more you give the Divine Itself corporeal expression, time and place in ways that can only happen in the context of your particular life of being and doing on Earth.

3/21 - 25	1	VEHUIAH—Will & New Beginnings
3/26 - 30	2	JELIEL—Love & Wisdom
3/31—4/4	3	SITAEL—Construction of Worlds
4/5—9	4	ELEMIAH—Divine Power
4/10—14	5	MAHASIAH—Rectification
4/15—20	6	LELAHEL—Light of Understanding
4/21—25	7	ACHAIAH—Patience
4/26—30	8	CAHETEL—Divine Blessings
5/1—5	9	HAZIEL—Divine Mercy & Forgiveness
5/6—10	10	ALADIAH—Divine Grace
5/11—15	11	LAUVIAH—Victory
5/16—20	12	HAHAIAH—Refuge/Shelter
5/21—25	13	YEZALEL—Fidelity, Loyalty, Allegiance
5/26—31	14	MEBAHEL—Truth, Liberty, Justice
6/1—5	15	HARIEL—Purification
6/6—10	16	HAKAMIAH—Loyalty

6/11—15	17 LAVIAH—Revelation
6/16—21	18 CALIEL—Justice
6/22—26	19 LEUVIAH—Expansive Intelligence, Fruition
6/27—7/1	20 PAHALIAH—Redemption
7/2—6	21 NELCHAEL—Ardent Desire to Learn
7/7—11	22 YEIAYEL—Fame/Renown
7/12—16	23 MELAHEL—Healing Capacity
7/17—22	24 HAHEUIAH—Protection
7/23—27	25 NITH-HAIAH—Spiritual Wisdom & Magic
7/28—8/1	26 HAAIAH—Political Science & Ambition
8/2—6	27 YERATEL—Propagation of the Light
8/7—12	28 SEHEIAH—Longevity
8/13—17	29 REIYEL—Liberation
8/18—22	30 OMAEL—Fertility, Multiplicity
8/23—28	31 LECABEL—Intellectual Talent
8/29—9/2	32 VASARIAH—Clemency & Equilibrium
9/3—7	33 YEHUIAH—Subordination to Higher Order
9/8—12	34 LEHAHIAH—Obedience
9/13—17	35 CHAVAKIAH—Reconciliation
9/18—23	36 MENADEL—Inner/Outer Work
9/24—28	37 ANIEL—Breaking the Circle
9/29—10/3	38 HAAMIAH—Ritual & Ceremony
10/4—8	39 REHAEL—Filial Submission
10/9—13	40 YEIAZEL—Divine Consolation & Comfort
10/14—18	41 HAHAHEL—Mission
10/19—23	42 MIKAEL—Political Authority & Order
10/24—28	43 VEULIAH—Prosperity
10/29—11/2	44 YELAHIAH—Karmic Warrior
11/3—7	45 SEALIAH—Motivation & Willfulness
11/8—12	46 ARIEL—Perceiver & Revealer
11/13—17	47 ASALIAH —Contemplation
11/18—22	48 MIHAEL—Fertility & Fruitfulness
11/23—27	49 VEHUEL—Elevation & Grandeur
11/28—12/2	50 DANIEL— Eloquence
12/3—7	51 HAHASIAH—Universal Medicine
12/8—12	52 IMAMIAH—Expiation of Errors
12/13—16	53 NANAEL—Spiritual Communication
12/17—21	54 NITHAEL—Rejuvenation & Eternal Youth
12/22—26	55 MEBAHIAH—Intellectual Lucidity
12/27—1/31	56 POYEL—Fortune & Support

1/1—5	57 NEMAMIAH—Discernment
1/6—10	58 YEIALEL—Mental Force
1/11—15	59 HARAHEL—Intellectual Richness
1/16—20	60 MITZRAEL—Internal Reparation
1/21—25	61 UMABEL—Affinity & Friendship
1/26—30	62 IAH-HEL—Desire to Know
1/31—2/4	63 ANAUEL—Perception of Unity
2/5—9	64 MEHIEL—Vivification (Invigorate/Enliven)
2/10—14	65 DAMABIAH—Fountain of Wisdom
2/15—19	66 MANAKEL—Knowledge of Good & Evil
2/20—24	67 EYAEL—Transformation to Sublime
2/25—29	68 HABUHIAH—Healing
3/1—5	69 ROCHEL—Restitution
3/6—10	70 JABAMIAH—Alchemy (Transformation)
3/11—15	71 HAIYAEL—Divine Warrior & Weaponry
3/16—20	72 MUMIAH—Endings & Rebirth

The 72 Angels' Times of Intellect Support

The following shows all 72 Angels in their one 20-minute period in the 24-hour day when they support the intellect plane, and thus express particular qualities of Divine Mind in your human intellect to help you cultivate awareness and higher-mind. Your Intellect Angel is the one who was governing within the 20-minute period of your birth at your place of birth. Thus, if you were born at 12:10 a.m. in California or London, your Intellect Angel would be 1 VEHUIAH. Those born at a cusp time—on the hour or 20 minutes before or after—may be said to have two Intellect Angels; so if you were born at 12:20 a.m., your two Intellect Angels would be 1 VEHUIAH and 2 JELIEL—or you may want to work with the one with which you feel the most resonance. Likewise if your time of birth is very close to a cusp time, for example 11:18 or 11:21 (11:20 would be the cusp for the preceding and upcoming Angel). Many people do not know their exact time of birth, so it is suggested in this case as well that as you become more acquainted with the 72 Angels, explore working with the Angel that most resonates for you during its time of Intellect support.

12 Midnight (a.m.) to 12 Noon (p.m.) (00:00—12:00)

12:00—12:20	1 VEHUIAH—Will & New Beginnings
12:20—12:40	2 JELIEL—Love & Wisdom
12:40—1:00	3 SITAEL—Construction of Worlds
1:00—1:20	4 ELEMIAH—Divine Power

1:20—1:40	5	MAHASIAH—Rectification
1:40—2:00	6	LELAHEL—Light of Understanding
2:00—2:20	7	ACHAIAH—Patience
2:20—2:40	8	CAHETEL—Divine Blessings
2:40—3:00	9	HAZIEL—Divine Mercy & Forgiveness
3:00—3:20	10	ALADIAH—Divine Grace
3:20—3:40	11	LAUVIAH—Victory
3:40—4:00	12	HAHAIAH—Refuge/Shelter
4:00—4:20	13	YEZALEL—Fidelity, Loyalty, Allegiance
4:20—4:40	14	MEBAHEL—Truth, Liberty, Justice
4:40—5:00	15	HARIEL—Purification
5:00—5:20	16	HAKAMIAH—Loyalty
5:20—5:40	17	LAVIAH—Revelation
5:40—6:00	18	CALIEL—Justice
6:00—6:20	19	LEUVIAH—Expansive Intelligence, Fruition
6:20—6:40	20	PAHALIAH—Redemption
6:40—7:00	21	NELCHAEL—Ardent Desire to Learn
7:00—7:20	22	YEIAYEL—Fame/Renown
7:20—7:40	23	MELAHEL—Healing Capacity
7:40—8:00	24	HAHEUIAH—Protection
8:00—8:20	25	NITH-HAIAH—Spiritual Wisdom & Magic
8:20—8:40	26	HAAIAH—Political Science & Ambition
8:40—9:00	27	YERATEL—Propagation of the Light
9:00—9:20	28	SEHEIAH—Longevity
9:20—9:40	29	REIYEL—Liberation
9:40—10:00	30	OMAEL—Fertility, Multiplicity
10:00—10:20	31	LECABEL—Intellectual Talent
10:20—10:40	32	VASARIAH—Clemency & Equilibrium
10:40—11:00	33	YEHUIAH—Subordination to Higher Order
11:00—11:20	34	LEHAHIAH—Obedience
11:20—11:40	35	CHAVAKIAH—Reconciliation
11:40—12:00	36	MENADEL—Inner/Outer Work

12:00 Noon (p.m.) to 12 Midnight (a.m.) (12:00—24:00)

12:00—12:20	37	ANIEL—Breaking the Circle
12:20—12:40	38	HAAMIAH—Ritual & Ceremony
12:40—1:00	39	REHAEL—Filial Submission
1:00—1:20	40	YEIAZEL—Divine Consolation & Comfort
1:20—1:40	41	HAHAHEL—Mission
1:40—2:00	42	MIKAEL—Political Authority & Order

2:00—2:20	43 VEULIAH—Prosperity
2:20—2:40	44 YELAHIAH—Karmic Warrior
2:40—3:00	45 SEALIAH—Motivation & Willfulness
3:00—3:20	46 ARIEL—Perceiver & Revealer
3:20—3:40	47 ASALIAH —Contemplation
3:40—4:00	48 MIHAEL—Fertility & Fruitfulness
4:00—4:20	49 VEHUEL—Elevation & Grandeur
4:20—4:40	50 DANIEL— Eloquence
4:40—5:00	51 HAHASIAH—Universal Medicine
5:00—5:20	52 IMAMIAH—Expiation of Errors
5:20—5:40	53 NANAEL—Spiritual Communication
5:40—6:00	54 NITHAEL—Rejuvenation & Eternal Youth
6:00—6:20	55 MEBAHIAH—Intellectual Lucidity
6:20—6:40	56 POYEL—Fortune & Support
6:40—7:00	57 NEMAMIAH—Discernment
7:00—7:20	58 YEIALEL—Mental Force
7:20—7:40	59 HARAHEL—Intellectual Richness
7:40—8:00	60 MITZRAEL—Internal Reparation
8:00—8:20	61 UMABEL—Affinity & Friendship
8:20—8:40	62 IAH-HEL—Desire to Know
8:40—9:00	63 ANAUEL—Perception of Unity
9:00—9:20	64 MEHIEL—Vivification (Invigorate/Enliven)
9:20—9:40	65 DAMABIAH—Fountain of Wisdom
9:40—10:00	66 MANAKEL—Knowledge of Good & Evil
10:00—10:20	67 EYAEL—Transformation to Sublime
10:20—10:40	68 HABUHIAH—Healing
10:40—11:00	69 ROCHEL—Restitution
11:00—11:20	70 JABAMIAH—Alchemy (Transformation)
11:20—11:40	71 HAIYAEL—Divine Warrior & Weaponry
11:40—12:00	72 MUMIAH—Endings & Rebirth

The 72 Angels' Correspondence to Degrees of the Zodiac

Medieval Kabbalists working with the 72 Angels corresponded their periods of governing to 360 degrees of the Zodiac, as shown below. The degrees correspondence was based on a lunar calendar of 360 days (12 months x 30 days), plus 5 days tacked on to reconcile the solar seasons, which several ancient civilizations observed (Maya, Aztec, India, Sumeria, Babylonia, Egypt, Hebrews, etc). Ultimately, most civilizations adhered to a calendar which combines the lunar cycles (354-day year) and solar seasons (365 + 1 days) by distributing the extra five days to various months of the 12-month lunar year, plus one additional leap year day every four years. According to Chabad.org, the centuries old Jewish calendar, still observed today, is considered to be a "Luni-Solar" calendar which adds a 13ᵗʰ month every so often for a "leap year."

Of course, 365 days don't fit perfectly into 360 degrees, so the 365-day calendar correspondences for the 72 Angels involve some overlapping of days. If you are an astrologer or astronomer you will know that because the Earth's orbit is elliptical, there are variations every year with degrees and days. Therefore, if your Birth Angels' dates of governing fall on or near the first or last day of a date or degree correspondence, you may also feel an affinity with the Angel before or after yours.

0° - 5° Aries	1 VEHUIAH—Will & New Beginnings
5° - 10° Aries	2 JELIEL—Love & Wisdom
10° - 15° Aries	3 SITAEL—Construction of Worlds
15° to 20° Aries	4 ELEMIAH—Divine Power
20° to 25° Aries	5 MAHASIAH—Rectification
25° to 30° Aries	6 LELAHEL—Light of Understanding
0° to 5° Taurus	7 ACHAIAH—Patience
5° to 10° Taurus	8 CAHETEL—Divine Blessings
10° to 15° Taurus	9 HAZIEL—Divine Mercy & Forgiveness
15° to 20° Taurus	10 ALADIAH—Divine Grace
20° to 25° Taurus	11 LAUVIAH—Victory
25° to 30° Taurus	12 HAHAIAH—Refuge, Shelter
0° to 5° Gemini	13 YEZALEL—Fidelity, Loyalty, Allegiance
5° to 10° Gemini	14 MEBAHEL—Truth, Liberty, Justice
10° to 15° Gemini	15 HARIEL—Purification
15° to 20° Gemini	16 HAKAMIAH—Loyalty
20° to 25° Gemini	17 LAVIAH—Revelation
25° to 30° Gemini	18 CALIEL—Justice
0° to 5° Cancer	19 LEUVIAH—Expansive Intelligence, Fruition
5° to 10° Cancer	20 PAHALIAH—Redemption
10° to 15° Cancer	21 NELCHAEL—Ardent Desire to Learn
15° to 20° Cancer	22 YEIAYEL—Fame, Renown
20° to 25° Cancer	23 MELAHEL—Healing Capacity
25° to 30° Cancer	24 HAHEUIAH—Protection
0° to 5° Leo	25 NITH-HAIAH—Spiritual Wisdom & Magic
5° to 10° Leo	26 HAAIAH—Political Science & Ambition
10° to 15° Leo	27 YERATEL—Propagation of the Light
15° to 20° Leo	28 SEHEIAH—Longevity
20° to 25° Leo	29 REIYEL—Liberation
25° to 30° Leo	30 OMAEL—Fertility, Multiplicity

0° to 5° Virgo	31 LECABEL—Intellectual Talent
5° to 10° Virgo	32 VASARIAH—Clemency & Equilibrium
10° to 15° Virgo	33 YEHUIAH—Subordination to Higher Order
15° to 20° Virgo	34 LEHAHIAH—Obedience
20° to 25° Virgo	35 CHAVAKIAH—Reconciliation
25° to 30° Virgo	36 MENADEL—Inner/Outer Work
0° to 5° Libra	37 ANIEL—Breaking the Circle
5° to 10° Libra	38 HAAMIAH—Ritual & Ceremony
10° to 15° Libra	39 REHAEL—Filial Submission
15° to 20° Libra	40 YEIAZEL—Divine Consolation & Comfort
20° to 25° Libra	41 HAHAHEL—Mission
25° to 30° Libra	42 MIKAEL—Political Authority & Order
0° to 5° Scorpio	43 VEULIAH—Prosperity
5° to 10° Scorpio	44 YELAHIAH—Karmic Warrior
10° to 15° Scorpio	45 SEALIAH—Motivation & Willfulness
15° to 20° Scorpio	46 ARIEL—Perceiver & Revealer
20° to 25° Scorpio	47 ASALIAH —Contemplation
25° to 30° Scorpio	48 MIHAEL—Fertility & Fruitfulness
0° to 5° Sagittarius	49 VEHUEL—Elevation & Grandeur
5° to 10° Sagittarius	50 DANIEL— Eloquence
10° to 15° Sagittarius	51 HAHASIAH—Universal Medicine
15° to 20° Sagittarius	52 IMAMIAH—Expiation of Errors
20° to 25° Sagittarius	53 NANAEL—Spiritual Communication
25° to 30° Sagittarius	54 NITHAEL—Rejuvenation & Eternal Youth
0° to 5° Capricorn	55 MEBAHIAH—Intellectual Lucidity
5° to 10° Capricorn	56 POYEL—Fortune & Support
10° to 15° Capricorn	57 NEMAMIAH—Discernment
15° to 20° Capricorn	58 YEIALEL—Mental Force
20° to 25° Capricorn	59 HARAHEL—Intellectual Richness
25° to 30° Capricorn	60 MITZRAEL—Internal Reparation
0° to 5° Aquarius	61 UMABEL—Affinity & Friendship
5° to 10° Aquarius	62 IAH-HEL—Desire to Know
10° to 15° Aquarius	63 ANAUEL—Perception of Unity
15° to 20° Aquarius	64 MEHIEL—Vivification (Invigorate/Enliven)
20° to 25° Aquarius	65 DAMABIAH—Fountain of Wisdom
25° to 30° Aquarius	66 MANAKEL—Knowledge of Good & Evil
0° to 5° Pisces	67 EYAEL—Transformation to Sublime
5° to 10° Pisces	68 HABUHIAH—Healing
10° to 15° Pisces	69 ROCHEL—Restitution
15° to 20° Pisces	70 JABAMIAH—Alchemy (Transformation)
20° to 25° Pisces	71 HAIYAEL—Divine Warrior & Weaponry
25° to 30° Pisces	72 MUMIAH—Endings & Rebirth

Appendix II

A Summary of
the 72 Angels' Roles in our Lives

From our religions, spiritual traditions and the multitude of Angelic experiences of individuals through the ages, much of humanity believes that the heavens are full of Angels who were created by God and Divinely charged to act as messengers, guides, guardians, helpers and protectors for us during our time on Earth. There is a softness in our hearts for Angels, because they don't bring us the laws of religion—but rather the love of the Divine for the human. The ancient Angelic Kabbalah introduces us to a kind of Angel that does all that—and so much more.

The millennia-old (at least) tradition of the 72 Angels of the Tree of Life resurfaced during the 20th century at a time in history when individual and collective consciousness could perhaps better receive its "practical mysticism." As a remarkable spiritual tool for self-discovery and personal transformation, this tradition reveals the powerful 72-member "host" of the Angelic-Divine, whose light-energies dwell within us to amplify our inner Divine and help us to realize and ultimately embody the deeper truth, potential and purpose of our Divine-Human beingness.

The 72 Angels of the Tree of Life are presented through centuries of Kabbalah mysticism not as *creations*, but as the initial *light-emanations* of the Divine Itself. It is said that in "the Beginning," the One—in Its great desire to know and express Itself—differentiated, or refracted, into 72 distinctive "angles" of light which revealed the inherent and paradoxical diversity of its Oneness. Fast forward to Creation and human life, these 72 Angelic Aspects—also referred to as "Faces," "Names" and Light-qualities of the Divine Being—are also said to be <u>expressed within, and through, the diversity of humanity</u>. Hence our "image and likeness" to the Divine, which is awakened and amplified by interaction with our inner Angelic "soulmates."

These teachings have their earliest foundation in the ancient oral traditions of mystical Judaism going back at least to the times of Abraham and Moses, which were passed down as secret knowledge through the Rabbinic generations. These include the mystical "creation codes" in the ancient *Sefer Yetzirah, (Book of Creation),* from the 3rd-6th centuries, arguably attributed to Abraham, among others; the "hidden knowledge" received by Moses that was not revealed when the Ten

Commandments were given to his people; and other revelatory sources from not only Jewish mysticism but also from Christian Cabalists, Gnostic mysticism, Sufism, Neoplatonists, the spiritual art and science of alchemy, and more. I have especially noted that in the Judeo-Christian Bible, there are certain Biblical references to the "Angels of the Presence," which came forth on the "first day" and were said to represent "the faces of God." Later, from a Hebrew decoding of the Bible's *Exodus*, chapter 14, verses 19-21, the 72 Angels' names were discerned as the 72 Names of God.

The Angelic Tree of Life. Tracing the Tree of Life symbology back at least to Isaac the Blind in the 12th century, Kabbalists worked through the Middle Ages and early Renaissance with the Tree of Life as a universal flow chart for Divine Self-Revelation through descending waves of energy, or emanations, which revealed the diverse aspects of Itself. The Tree symbology shows that from the Unknowable Divine "No-Thingness" and "No-Thingness without End" ("Ain" and "Ain Sof") emerged the "Ain Sof Aur" of Never-Ending Light. From this great Divine Light emanated the 72 Angels as *angles*, or refractions, of Light through the first Nine of the "Ten Sephirot," the "Four Planes of Existence," the Elements and more. Thereby the "many" within the One was revealed—setting the cosmic stage for the Creation of all diverse things and beings.

In the hierarchies of Divine Emanation, each emanation contained the attributes of all that came before it, plus something newly revealed—just as in the generations of created beings. Thus, the Tree of Life is also a template for universal man, "Adam Kadmon," and the mysteries of the Divine-Human two-way relationship that plays out in all our being and doing on Earth. Kabbalists tell us that the 72 Angels are "key connectors" in our relationship with the Divine. 20th century Kabbalist Omraan Mikhael Aivanhov (1900-1986) called the 72 Angels "stepdown transformers," bringing the energies of the Divine to the human, and he also referred to them the "edible fruits of the Tree of Life." For it is said that as we partake of them, our image and likeness to the Divine is increased. By imbibing the Angelic Energies, we become Divine. *This puts the ultimate positive spin on "you are what you eat!"*

The Roles of the 72 Angels in Human Life. The foundational premise of the Angelic Kabbalah and the 72 Angels tradition is that God is within us and we are within God, and thus both the Divine and the Human are evolving and expanding together through our unique Divine-Human beingness and continual co-creation of life on Earth. The role of the 72 Angels is to work with, within and among us to awaken our soul-awareness and amplify our inner Divine so that we become empowered beyond the seeming limitations of matter, time and place for the greater fulfillment of our soul purposes and potentials on Earth.

Even as the 72 Angels represent the vast spectrum of Divine possibilities and purposes within our humanity, our personal "Birth Angels" amplify a particular configuration of Divine qualities with which we are more deeply endowed, which illuminate who we uniquely are and support our challenges and potentials in all we are here to heal, express and manifest in our current lifetime. Simply put, working with our Birth Angels helps us to know and become more of who we are by bringing our inner soul-identity into our outer being and doing.

Thus the 72 Angels, and our personal Birth Angels, are said to serve us in these ways:

As "angles" and amplifiers of light-consciousness and the awareness that we are not "only human," but Divine-Human beings. The 72 Angels show us that God is everywhere, in the inside and outside of everything and everyone as not only the animating Spirit of physical matter—but also physical matter itself as denser vibrations of Divine Light. Thus, God, and all that is Divine, is not separate and apart from us, but rather here within, and *as*, each of us as a differentiated soul-spark of Itself that gives particular meaning, purpose and spiritual essence to our human form. For just as the 72 Angels, as *angles* of Divine Light, each express particular details of the Divine "I AM" as "I AM THAT WHICH," they also help us to express the I AM of the Divine through, and as, our own Divine-Human being and doing.

As illuminators of the Love and Truth which compose and expand our Divine-Human nature and tell the whole story of who we are. The 72 Angels show us that we are each here to root particular qualities of Divine Love and Truth on Earth through the loves and truths of who we are and what we dream to be and do. This is why there is so much energy and momentum around our earthly endeavors and creations that are propelled by "doing what we love and loving what we do." For it is only love that knows the whole story of who we are in both time and eternity. Only love gives us endless second chances for any moment in which we may fall short of our potential. Only love, from within us and around us, grows the truth of us, ever inspiring and inviting us to bring more and more of who we truly are into being.

As "heart-bridge" builders within us and two-way messengers between our own Divine and human aspects and the greater totality of Spirit. Spiritual wisdoms through the ages have told us that the heart is "a meeting place between the human and the Divine." Likewise, the 72 Angels use the sacred human heart as a bridge between soul and body—amplifying and transmitting into our heart the Divine qualities and purposes imprinted within our soul, and from there into our mind/body preoccupations, expressions and actions. In other words, the Angels help the soul talk to the heart, and the heart to talk to mind and body.

As the Angels amplify our soul-light, the Divine qualities and purposes held in our soul are broadcast into our heart as love, compassion, intuition and personal truth—and then the Angels help to "turn up the volume" in the heart so that mind and body can hear. Looking at the Angels, and ourselves, in this light, we can perhaps consider that our inner voice of truth and intuition is the Angelic Divine guiding us not from "above" or afar, but right here, from within our own soul-infused heart. In addition, because of the heart's capacity for love, compassion, understanding and wisdom-making, the knowledge and experience we bring into our heart can be mined by our soul for the "sharing" of our human experience with the totality of the Divine Itself— as well as with the collective human consciousness—while at the same time expanding our Divine-Human potential here on Earth.

Furthermore, of crucial importance to our personal well-being and that of the whole planet is that the heart is not only where the light-seeds of our individuation are held, but also, paradoxically where our unity-connection to our fellow beings and all of Creation may be experienced. Thus the heart is, as Siddha Yoga guru Nityananda said, "the hub of all sacred places," a "fulcrum of the cosmos" (Upanishads), and a two-way bridge that connects "a causal link" between and among Spirit-soul-self-others (Aryeh Kaplan's commentary on the *Sefer Yetzirah*). Through our connected hearts, we can realize the oneness which we are all, each in our unique and diverse ways, continually expressing as the many within the One and the One within the many.

In prayer, meditation and communication with the Divine, we are doing two marvelous things—(1) quickening our awareness that we have the rarer ethers of the Divine "on tap" within our own heart and soul for communion and help with our human-life conditions and circumstances, and that (2) by plugging into our own inner Divine, we gain access to the totality of the Divine in the collective consciousness of all Creation and the cosmos—and the compounded spiritual magic that can occur "when two or more are gathered!" This is why prayer-chains, group meditations and healings are so powerful.

As transmuters of our "shadow" energies and transformers of our base mettle into "Divine-Human gold." The 72 Angels, as "agents of personal transformation," have long been associated with the spiritual art and science of alchemy. In amplifying particular qualities of Divine Light within us for healing our accumulated karma of harbored hurts, issues and transgressions against self and others, the Angels stimulate the "base mettle" of our humanity to be transformed into the spiritual gold of Divine consciousness. Thereby we may be free to fulfill our Divine-Human potential and express the dharma of our soul purposes in service to ourselves, each other and the Divine Itself within, and as, who we uniquely are.

As the Wisdoms suggest, we are not meant to do battle with our inner shadows, but to "bring them to light" so that we may know where healing is needed. The 72 Angels are said to be especially equipped for this because they each have their own "shadow counterpart," represented by the "Inversions" of their "Virtues," which is also implied by the number 144 associated with them. (See the first *Birth Angels* book at amazon.com or 72BirthAngels.com for the 72 Angels' Inversions.)

Although the duality of the world brings us both the light and the dark, when we are willing to confront the shadows within us, the shadows in the outer world ultimately have no dominion over us. In the Angelic mysteries, the more love-and-truth light we allow to expand within us, the less room there is for hurt, doubt, worry, shame, guilt or any thought or feeling which causes us to diminish rather than expand. Ultimately, as heart-and-soul awareness saturates our being with Divine consciousness, our human aspects are ennobled and the vibrations of our entire being are heightened. This is ascension in the body—the divinization of our humanity and the means by which we may fulfill the desire of the Divine within us to bring the heavens to Earth and experience life through us, as only each of us can live it.

As expressions of the inherently diverse nature of the Divine Oneness within, and as, the diversity of our individual and collective humanity. As with the first Angelic light-emanations of the Divine which revealed Its inherent diversity *to Itself*, the 72 Angels illuminate and help us to embrace the diversity of qualities which compose our own Divine-Human nature and all the diverse expressions of Creation—and how in our diverse and complementary togetherness we can expand the potential of all. As the Wisdoms suggest, if we will ever have peace on Earth, we must come to understand that "*it takes the totality of humankind and the beings and things of the natural world and beyond to reveal and express the diverse nature of God.*" If we are truly made "in the image and likeness of the Divine," then to shun someone who is "different" is to shun not only an aspect of ourselves, but also that aspect of God. This suggests the importance of not just tolerating or merely accepting—but celebrating—each other's diversities as blessings for all of humanity. For truly, *if God is all there is*, then we are each here to literally "flesh out" our unique part of that Bigger Picture with the fullness of our particular being—for the fulfillment of ourselves, each other and the Divine on Earth.

This is the utopia of "Heaven on Earth" that is our Divine-Human destiny, if we dare. No matter how pervasive, or persuasive, the darkest days and nights of our individual and global happenings, we must continue to strive toward the "brighter Angels" that dwell within and among us, even for and *as* us. If we can realize that Divine Will is carried out through the love and truth of our own Divine-Human will, then we can, *if we will*, re-create the "Garden of Eden" on Earth within our collective hearts. For in the sameness of heart beneath all our outer differences is the longing of love to do so.

About the Author

TERAH COX has worked with the Kabbalah, Christianity, Sufism and aspects of other spiritual paths and wisdoms throughout her life in search of the common threads of Love and Truth in their mystical hearts. In addition to the five-volume series of *Birth Angels Book of Days*, she is the author of *Different Ships, Same Boat: Songs for the Soul of America; The Story of Love & Truth; A Love Your Heart Can Believe In; Birth Angels ~ Fulfilling Your Life Purpose with the 72 Angels of the Kabbalah; You Can Write Song Lyrics*, and more. She is also a speaker, guide and mentor on the Angelic Kabbalah and the subjects of "Truing-Up Your Life," individuation and work/purpose, sacred perspectives on diversity, inspiration, creativity and spiritual development. Drawing from the fruits of "extraordinary listening," she has used the various aspects of her work as ways to explore and share the Divine-Human mysteries at play within every being, circumstance and aspect of life.

Formerly a writer for the Aura-Soma Colour-Care-System® in the U.K., as well as a freelance writer across many fields, Terah was also a lyric writer (as Terry Cox) signed to Columbia Pictures, BMG, Warner-Chappell and various European music publishers, with over 150 songs recorded for CDs, film and television. In addition, her inspirational poetry-art designs for wall-art, greeting cards, prints and more are offered online and in retail shops across the U.S.

* * *

Books & materials, Birth Angels Consults & personal guidance:
www.72BirthAngels.com | www.TerahCox.com

Poetry and word-art, greeting cards, prints & more:
www.HeavenandEarthWorks.com

BIRTH ANGELS BOOK OF DAYS
Daily Wisdoms with the 72 Angels of the Tree of Life

Volume 1: March 21—June 2
Relationship with the Divine

Volume 2: June 3—August 16
Relationship with Self

Volume 3: August 17—October 29
Relationship with Work and Purpose

Volume 4: October 30—January 8
Relationship with Others

Volume 5: January 9—March 20
Relationship with Community and the World

———————————————

Additional Offerings on the Angelic Kabbalah

***Birth Angels ~ Fulfilling Your Life Purpose
with the 72 Angels of the Kabbalah***

"Daily Wisdoms" E-Mail Subscription

72 Angels Inspiration Cards

Birth Angels Consults

Quick-Reference Charts & Posters:
The Kabbalah Tree of Life
72 Angels Days & Hours of Support

———————————————

www.72BirthAngels.com | www.TerahCox.com

www.ingramcontent.com/pod-product-compliance
Lightning Source LLC
LaVergne TN
LVHW051255080426
835509LV00020B/2978